Silis Muhammad's United Nations Interventions on behalf of Afrodescendants

Unprecedented and historic research and study

BOOKS BY SILIS MUHAMMAD

In My Next Life

Reparations petition for United Nations assistance under Resolution 1503 (XLVIII) on behalf of African-Americans in the United States of America

Hear Silis: Illuminating the Lost-Found Nation of Islam

The Wake of the Nation of Islam

Silis Muhammad's United Nations Interventions on behalf of Afrodescendants

Unprecedented and historic research and study

Silis Muhammad

Lost-Found Nation of Islam
3040 Campbellton Road SW,
Atlanta, Georgia 30311

Silis Muhammad's United Nations Interventions on behalf of Afrodescendants

Copyright © 2020 by the Senate of the Afrodescendant Nation
Published by the Lost-Found Nation of Islam

All rights reserved. Published 2020.
Printed in the United States of America.

No parts of this publication may be reproduced, stored in a reproduced, stored, in a retrieval system, or transmitted in any form or by any means electronic, mechanical, photocopying, recording or otherwise without the prior written permission of the publisher.

ISBN: SC-9798780356349
ISBN: HC-9798780429685

Cover and Author photo by: onsite United Nation Photographer

Dedication

...To My People

The Afrodescendants

"Self-Determination is our right, Separation with all our might, Reparations is our fight."

Contents

Dedication	xi
Acknowledgments	xiii
Preface	xv
Oral Statement to the UN in 2008	1
Sub-Commission Conference Room Paper: A Regional Perspective on Afro-descendant Quality of Life (2006)	3
Written and Oral Statements to the UN in 2006	46
Written and Oral Statements to the UN in 2005	50
Written and Oral Statements to the UN in 2004	60
Written and Oral Statements to the UN in 2003	72
Written and Oral Statements to the UN in 2002	87
Written and Oral Statements to the UN in 2001	103
Oral Statements to Regional Seminars for Afrodescendants	119
Written and Oral Statements to the World Conference Against Racism	126
Written and Oral Statements to the UN in 2000	132

Written and Oral Statements to the UN in 1999		152

Written and Oral Statements to the UN in 1998		179

Written Statement to the UN in 1997		203

Petition for Reparations to the UN under 1503 Procedure

delivered in 1994		206

Acknowledgments

I would like to acknowledge all parties of the United Nations that opened their doors to leaders of the Afrodescendant Nation regarding our fight for Afrodescendant human rights and reparations; and Senator Abdullah Tahama, Senator Mahasin Mahdi, and Senator Karim Al-Haqq (peace be upon him) for the introduction of Senate Bill #120384-3 to protect and copyright my intellectual properties. Thank you Senator Mahasin Mahdi and Samina "Sunshine" Najmah for appreciating my work and collaborating with myself to construct a collection of my United Nation records of achievement regarding Afrodescendant human rights and reparations for slavery plantations.

Preface

The Honorable Silis Muhammad Expands His Record of Achievement in the Fight for Afrodescendant Human Rights and Reparations for Plantation Slavery

Mr. Muhammad's abbreviated list of United Nations (UN) interventions delivered in advancement of Afrodescendant human rights and reparations for plantation slavery is listed below:

- **1994 Petition for Reparations to the UN under 1503 Procedure** – Mr. Muhammad delivered a 1503 communication to the UN Working Group on Communications on behalf of African Americans.

- **1997 Written Statement to the UN** – Mr. Muhammad recommended opening a forum so that African-American human rights grievances, that formed the basis of a petition submitted, can be expressed systematically, as well as officially recorded, evaluated, and remedied.

- **1998 Written and Oral Statements** – Mr. Muhammad urged the Commission on Human Rights to assist African Americans in their efforts to recover from official U.S. policies of enslavement, apartheid, and forced assimilation. Mr. Muhammad prayed that the human rights of African Americans be recaptured politically and amicably, rights to self-determination rectified, and the damages sustained be awarded in great measure in order to accomplish the cathartic cleansing mentally, emotionally, and physically of 400 years of long-suffering. Mr. Muhammad prayed that the U.S. Government not be given the tacit approval of the UN to subvert the opening of a forum wherein African-American grievances can be expressed systematically, and officially recorded, evaluated and remedied.

- **1999 Written and Oral Statements** – Mr. Muhammad requested recognition of the African American choice of human rights and inalienable rights. He requested the crime of plantation slavery, and its lingering effects, be rectified–which was, and is still, a crime against African Americans and against humanity. Mr. Muhammad asked the U.N. to establish a forum for the purpose of restoring African American human rights, their political being, and their status as a people. Mr. Muhammad urged recommendation that the Sub-Commission pass a resolution recognizing slavery and the slave trade as a crime against humanity. He urged the writing of a working paper as a way to begin analyzing African American's situation. Mr. Muhammad urged African American inclusion in the Declaration on the Rights of Persons Belonging to National or Ethnic, Religious and Linguistic Minorities, or a new declaration be written for African Americans. Mr. Muhammad asked the International Labor Organization to look into America's privately owned prisons.

- **2000 Written and Oral Statements** – Mr. Muhammad asked that the U.S. pay reparations to the so-called African Americans, since the U.S. cannot restore the 'mother tongue' of African Americans if ever it wanted to. Mr. Muhammad recommended the U.S. be held liable, at the least, for the last 51 years, plus the additional years which are needed to resolve this issue. He asked that the UN place a reparation sanction upon America if the identity and language of minorities and Peoples are to be preserved. Mr. Muhammad asked that a precise dollar amount be given at a future date, if warranted, and that he stated that he would ask for the release of a number of African-American human rights victims who have been unjustly incarcerated in federal and state penitentiaries. Finally, Mr. Muhammad asked the UN to impose a sanction on the U.S. in the form of exemption from all taxation upon our people for as long as this issue is in the hands of the UN.

- **World Conference Against Racism Written and Oral Statements** – Mr. Muhammad recommended that the World Conference Against Racism declare a decade to consider the issues of slave descendants, including whether "LOST FOUND Peoples" is the term that best identifies slave descendants.

- **Regional Seminars for Afrodescendants Oral Statements** – Mr. Muhammad put forth the name Lost Found Peoples as a name in order to gain human rights protection for slave descendants, but the name Afrodescendants was agreed upon by unanimous consent.

- **2001 Written and Oral Statements** – Mr. Muhammad urged UN intervention to protect and assist African-American leaders within a forum as they seek to determine the damage they have sustained and the means of reparation needed in order to bring them back to life as a People. Mr. Muhammad prayed for reparations for the damage suffered during slavery, and asked the Commission on Human Rights to hear the African American demand for the right to choose to reconstitute, and reconstruct lost ties, since no international instruments, arbitrations, mechanisms or laws requiring the recognition of minorities that can restrain ethnic conflict during 2001. Attorney Harriet AbuBakr, Mr. Muhammad's wife, asked the Working Group on Minorities to cause minority protection to develop in accord with the African American needs for resurrection.

- **2002 Written and Oral Statements** – On behalf of African Americans, Mr. Muhammad asked the Sub-Commission on the Promotion and Protection of Human Rights to acknowledge the decision that African Americans be recognized as Afrodescendant Minorities. Mr. Muhammad also recommended that the Commission on Human Rights pass a resolution requesting that the Sub-Commission on the Promotion and Protection of Human Rights place African Americans on its agenda, alongside Indigenous Peoples and Minorities. Mr. Muhammad also put forth a prayer for official recognition of a self-chosen collective identity and reparations for African Americans.

- **2003 Written and Oral Statements** – Mr. Muhammad requested official recognition of new minorities, urged the establishment of an International Year for Minorities, requested support for the efforts of the Working Group on Minorities, and recommended that the Working Group on Minorities organize a second Regional Seminar for Afrodescendant Minorities. Attorney Abu Bakr asked the Working Group on Minorities to validate Afrodescendants self-chosen identity in its documents, and use any other means available to place the fact of the existence of Afrodescendants before the UN and the world.

- **2004 Written and Oral Statements** – Mr. Muhammad called upon the UN to grant Afrodescendants protected collective human rights. Mr. Muhammad also asked the Sub-Commission to make a commitment to minorities that their interventions will be heard. Mr. Muhammad requested the recognition, protection, and assistance of the Commission on Human Rights, and the authorities of the UN.

- **2005 Written and Oral Statements** – Mr. Muhammad recommended sanctions against all governments that have deprived Afrodescendants, for every day Afrodescendants have been so denied human rights. He also requested assistance to Afrodescendants in efforts to have a self-chosen identity recognized and protected by the entire UN and by the governments under which Afrodescendants live.

- **2006 Written and Oral Statements** – Mr. Muhammad requested formal UN recognition of slave descendant's self-chosen name, Afrodescendants, and requested restoration of slave descendants to the human families of the earth.

- **2008 Oral Statement** – Mr. Muhammad requested that the UN Working Group on Minorities assist Afrodescendants to establish education for Afrodescendants in their original (mother) tongue.

- **2014 Open Letter to U.S. President Barack Obama** – Mr. Muhammad sent a letter to U.S. President Obama, Congress, General Dempsey, and the Pope of Rome requesting reparations for Afrodescendants.

Oral Statement to the UN in 2008

Oral Statement to the Forum on Minority Issues, First Session, Agenda Item VI: The Relationship Between De-Segregation Strategies, Cultural Autonomy and Integration in the Quest for Social Cohesion, December 2008

Greetings Madam Chair, Madam Gay McDougall, Experts, Country Representatives, Scholars and Minorities:

One of the purposes of this Forum is the identification of challenges and problems facing minorities and States. We, Afrodescendants, want for ourselves and for our children an education, especially now at our inception as an internationally recognized human family. We want an education in our original (mother) tongue. UN scholars state that language, not just any language, but one's "mother tongue" is intimately bound with identity. Thus, the right to such an education is an identity right.

Article 1, Section 1.1 of the Declaration on the Rights of Persons Belonging to Minorities indicates States shall protect and promote the identity of minorities. The United States of America, mainly, as well as other States, have breached this United Nations obligation. Since the abolition of slavery until now, Afrodescendants have been denied self-identity: education in our mother tongue. It is the very dignity we are without. The former slave-holding States have a duty to protect not only the existence but the national, ethnic, cultural, religious and linguistic identity of Minorities.

Mr. M. Cherif Bassiouni stated, in his final report to the 56th session of the Commission on Human Rights, that economic compensation for victims of gross violations of human rights should be provided for any assessable damage resulting from violations of international human rights and humanitarian law: (b) lost opportunities, including education. Since we were forcibly deprived of our mother tongue due to slavery and its lingering effects, we want compensation from those States, especially the United States, responsible for denying us an education intimately bound with identity. Afrodescendants claim the right to compensation for violations of international law, articulated in the Declaration on the Rights of Minorities as well as Article 27 of the ICCPR, due to lost opportunities, including education.

In conclusion, we suggest that the regional forums for Afrodescendants, started under the auspices of the former Working Group on Minorities, be continued so that Afrodescendants can discuss practical, acceptable and adaptable solutions to the unique problems we face.

Thank you.

Mr. Silis Muhammad

Sub-Commission Conference Room Paper: A Regional Perspective on Afro-descendant Quality of Life (2006)

NOTE: Original Working Paper: A Regional Perspective on Afrodescendant Quality of Life
English / Spanish / Portuguese (2005)

Distr. RESTRICTED

A/HRC/Sub.1/58/AC.5/CRP.1 *
8 August 2006

ENGLISH ONLY

HUMAN RIGHTS COUNCIL
Sub-Commission on the Promotion and Protection of Human Rights
Fifty-eighth session
Working Group on Minorities
Twelfth session
Item 5 (c) of the provisional agenda

A Regional Perspective on Afrodescendant Quality of Life

Conference Room Paper by
All For Reparations and Emancipation (AFRE)
Presented by:
Harriett AbuBakr, Esq. and Silis Muhammad

Written by:

Ishmael Abdul-Salaam, Harriett AbuBakr, Esq., Amanda Furness, Ida Hakim-Lawrence, Silis Muhammad, Ajani Mukarram, Adib Siraj Nabawi, and Dr. Raymond Winbush

Translated by:
Norma Casas, Spanish and Flavio Concalves, Portuguese

---

* Pursuant to General Assembly resolution 60/251 of 15 March 2006 entitled "Human Rights Council", all mandates, mechanisms, functions and responsibilities of the Commission on Human Rights, including the Sub-Commission, were assumed, as of 19 June 2006, by the Human Rights Council. Consequently, the symbol series E/CN.4/Sub.2/_, under which the Sub-Commission reported to the former Commission on Human Rights, has been replaced by the series A/HRC/Sub.1/_ as of 19 June 2006.

Introduction

For centuries, the descendants of Africans enslaved in the Americas, herein referred to as Afrodescendants, have been subjected to numerous forms of discrimination in countries throughout the Trans-Atlantic Slavery Diaspora. From Jamaica to the United States, Cuba to Canada, Guyana to Guatemala, these individuals share a common thread…although their fathers may have come from a tribe in Cameroon and their mothers from a tribe in Nigeria, making them indeed African people, they are unlike other people of African descent around the world in that they cannot use their mother tongue to call upon any government in Africa for support. Through forced mixed breeding they were deprived of their mother tongue and thereby they are denied the use of it today. Due to slavery's lingering effects they speak the language of their slave masters—be it English, Spanish, Portuguese or a mixed language. This communal history is a determining factor in the quality of life of Afrodescendant communities, underlying the poverty, inadequate health care and unequal access to opportunity that Afrodescendants suffer in the states in which they reside today.

Discrimination against Afrodescendants has historically manifested itself in each nation in various ways, and to varying degrees. Still, in most cases, it is born out of a Euro-centric sense of racial, cultural, economic and intellectual superiority, and out of a fear of retribution for the indignities suffered during and as a result of slavery. Those identifying as "white" commonly afford themselves higher social standing than is permitted the descendants of slaves, in part because of Afrodescendant's slave ancestry itself. With ancestors who were severed from their mother tongue and cultural roots upon being kidnapped, Afrodescendants in the Western Hemisphere today cannot—except in very rare cases—claim tribal membership, point of ancestral origin, language, land rights or equality nor may they enjoy the benefits of their forefather's labors or experience true human equality. This is despite the fact that enslaved persons were responsible for building much of the infrastructure that presently exists in their respective nations, and for establishing the bulk of agriculture as well. In the state of Georgia (US), taxes charged on each slave were used to fund the state government's initial treasury.1

In many states, similar forms of exploitation and unjust enrichment were—and continue to be— implemented and used. Even in nations where Afrodescendants may constitute a numerical majority, they are shown to possess less wealth and political power than those of other races because of such discriminatory practices.

Overall, the lingering effects of slavery and race-based discrimination have had an allencompassing, profoundly negative effect on the descendants of African slaves. Many nations are unaware of the difficulties facing this group, even within the constraints of their own borders. This paper seeks to spread awareness about the multitude of issues that currently face Afrodescendants in the Americas region, by attempting to highlight several factors within the context of this work, among them: the number of Afrodescendants in various countries, examples of discrimination against Afrodescendants and the economic and social conditions that result from such discrimination.

It should be noted that the study of Afrodescendants as a group is merely in its beginning stage, that acquiring accurate information on population numbers is still difficult and that this paper is in its initial form, to be completed in full at a later date. Some reports cited in this work may combine

Afrodescendant and African immigrant populations together into one overarching

category. Others may not contain accurate information for various reasons, among them a reluctance on the part of individuals to identify as a slave descendant because of the perception of shame attached to such a claim. This paper attempts to accomplish no more than to substantiate the collective existence of Afrodescendants as a group and to lay the groundwork for future study regarding their collective quality of life; issues of identification would be addressed in subsequent research.

It is hoped that through the efforts of the Working Group on Minorities and other concerned parties, Afrodescendant populations throughout the Slavery Diaspora will be offered a forum in which to share like experiences with one another and with the international community. Such a forum could be useful in establishing effective networks and thus initiatives that will advocate for Afrodescendant issues on a regional and, later, global scale. The legacy that members of this group share is one that Afrodescendants alone can uniquely lay claim to; it is a portion of world history and an experience of collective human rights abuses that deserves to be examined and explored by international bodies, at the very least.

The Scattering

An estimated 27,233 slave voyages arrived in the New World during the period of time ranging from 1492 to 1820, each new arrival bearing between 281 to 332 slaves.[2] These estimates fail to take into account the large numbers of slaves who were shuffled between various African nations, and who were taken to Europe, India and the Middle East. Information regarding Afrodescendant groups in these regions will be compiled during future research.

In the Americas, enslaved Africans disembarked at numerous ports throughout the region, and though many were held captive in areas close to the point from where they initially disembarked, many more were taken into the interiors of various nations, by boat or across land. The Cambridge Trans-Atlantic Slave Trade Database estimates 482 separate ports of arrival for these voyages in the Americas region; the listing of ports in itself is an overwhelming glimpse of how spread out and vast the trade actually was.

The above-cited data provides a framework for illustrating the dispersion of Africans into various nations. Although some estimates are much higher, scholars agree that at a minimum, between 12-15 million Africans were taken into slavery, where they were scattered throughout what has become known as the Slavery Diaspora; it was during this period of dispersion that most found themselves transplanted by force into societies both foreign and hostile.

Historical Overview and Current Population Estimates

Northern America

Since there has been no census category established for Afrodescendants in the U.S. and Canada, accurate population counts do not yet exist. African immigrants and their descendants are encouraged to register themselves under the racial/ethnic categories of African-Canadian, African-American or Black alongside Afrodescendants who also choose these categories. While scholars are well aware that a loss of national identity and the lingering effects of slavery differentiate Afrodescendants from African immigrants and their descendants, most governments have yet to acknowledge the distinction. It may be beneficial, in the future, for governments and

NGOs to identify the differences in the quality of life of Afrodescendants and African immigrants and their children, with an eye toward analyzing the how the destruction of original identity has disadvantaged Afrodescendants specifically.

The first enslaved Africans are believed to have disembarked at Jamestown, Virginia (U.S.) in 16193 , although some Black leaders have argued with that date, asserting that the first ship carrying slaves arrived in 1555, piloted by Sir John Hawkins. Until 1865, Africans in the U.S. were enslaved, tortured and denied even the most basic of human freedoms. In that year, slavery was abolished, only to be replaced with segregation laws that further denied the humanity of the freed slaves and their descendants. These laws were enforced by state mandate until 1954, when the United States Supreme Court outlawed the notion of 'separate but equal,' calling for integration of the nation's public school systems. Despite the Court's mandate, Afrodescendants in the United States have been— and still are—subjected to sub-human treatment by their own government and by the society that surrounds them. Researchers at the Tuskegee Institute note that between the years of 1882 and 1951, 3,437 Afrodescendants were lynched.4 In the U.S., hate crimes committed against Afrodescendants continue on, as illustrated in the 1991 beating of Rodney King by Los Angeles police officers, the beating and dragging death of James Byrd by white supremacists in Texas in 1998, and the shooting death of Robert Spencer in 2001. The father of eight children, Spencer was murdered as he left a Lake County, Florida convenience store by a man whose admitted goal was to "take out" as many black people as he could.5

According to the 2005 U.S. Census, 38.4 million people in the United States or 12.9% of the total population identify as Black, African-American or Afrodescendant. Fifty-five percent of the current Afrodescendant population in the U.S. resides in the nation's Southern region, where plantation slavery began and was the most entrenched. There are several instances in the United States of Afrodescendant groups who have remained on the land worked by their ancestors, among them the Gullahs of South Carolina and the Georgia Sea Islands. Today, groups like the Gullahs struggle to hold on to their land, which their respective states continue to encroach upon.

The Black Exodus to Canada initially occurred in three phases; it is estimated that over 35,000 fled north in search of respite. Fabbi notes that "the majority of early Black immigrants came as a result of three significant American historical events: the American Revolution (1775-1783), the War of 1812 (1812-1814), and the Underground Railway movement (1830-1865)."6 These migrations northward to freedom—combined with African immigration—have resulted in a current Canadian African/Afrodescendant population of 662, 200, representing just over 2% of Canada's total population. Despite Canada's historically significant role in the Underground Railroad as a place of safety for escaped slaves, many Afrodescendants in Canada today find that they face discriminatory circumstances and have been remanded to the outer levels of Canadian society.

Latin America

Vinson states that between the years of 1521 and 1817, Mexico imported almost 200,000 Africans to be used as slaves. These blacks were forced to work in silver mines, the farming industry, and on tobacco and sugar plantations.8 Based upon data derived from the colonial period that places the percentage of Mexico's African population somewhere between 10 and 12 per cent of the total, researchers estimate that about 9 million Mexicans could have significant African blood. The country's political, business, social and cultural spheres, however, are

A/HRC/Sub.1/58/AC.5/CRP.1
page 5

dominated by the white descendants of Spanish conquistadors, while mixed-race, indigenous and black people generally are relegated to supporting roles in society."9 Afrodescendants, also referred to as Afro-mestizos, reside mainly along Mexico's coastline. Most Afrodescendant villages are located in remote regions, according to the African Diaspora Research Project of Michigan State University.

The Inter-American Development Bank estimates that approximately 150 million of Latin America's 540 million people are of African ancestry.10 Great numbers of African slaves were imported into the area during the colonial period, the highest percentage of enslaved residing in Brazil.

Brazil currently is home to the largest Afrodescendant population in the Americas. Forty-five percent of Brazilians identify themselves as Black, while in Colombia

Afrodescendants comprise 26% of the total population; Argentina, Guatemala, Peru and Uruguay have small Afrodescendant populations that are concentrated in specific geographic areas. Bolivia, Ecuador and Costa Rica, along with other nations, have only begun to include questions related to race on their censuses, which means that many Afrodescendants may have gone uncounted. The NGO, Minority Rights Group International, laments the lack of available data on Afrodescendants in their 2004 report, blaming a lack of communication between Afrodescendant groups and their respective governments for statistical oversights, along with the fact that Afrodescendants are only now—at this late date—being recognized as a group. This much-needed research, MRG claims, could be used to improve upon the lives and circumstances of Afrodescendants throughout the Western Hemisphere.

The descendants of enslaved Africans in Central and South America live in rural areas and along the coastline, though many are migrating to large cities looking for work. This is an enormous undertaking for most, as disproportionate numbers of Afrodescendants across Latin America suffer from a lack of transportation, infrastructure and utilities, and are regularly denied access to health care, receive inadequate education, struggle with high unemployment rates and earn low incomes that place them easily below poverty level. In many countries, Afrodescendants—also dubbed Afro-Ecuadorians, Afro-Latinos, Afro-Colombians, Quilombos, Garifunas, AfroPeruvians and Black Seminoles—constitute the lowest rung on the quality of life ladder. The Inter-American Development Bank undertook a survey of Afrodescendants in Honduras, Peru, Uruguay and Venezuela; the study's results showed an astounding similarity in group member's experiences, despite the divergence of nations.

The Caribbean

In Haiti, the Dominican Republic and Cuba, Afrodescendants are the majority. Explorer Christopher Columbus first stumbled upon the island of Hispanola in 1492. Spanish colonial rule meant that between the period of 1492 and 1821, large numbers of African slaves were brought to the island, which has borne several names, among them Ayiti, Hispanola, Saint Domingue and finally—after the nation's 1821 revolution—Haiti. The island proved to be the most profitable in the region for its colonial holders, but for Africans and their descendants, Haiti was one of the most brutal places in the New World in terms of the slave trade and its resulting legacy. Library of Congress researchers claim that modern Haitian

society—with its violence and conflict, poverty and rapidly declining quality of life—is a direct reflection of the nation's slaveholding history.

"The mixture of races that eventually divided Haiti into a small, mainly mulatto elite and an impoverished black majority, began with the slavemasters' concubinage of African women. Haiti's slave population totaled at least 500,000, and perhaps as many as 700,000, by 1791. The slaveholding system in Saint-Domingue was particularly cruel and abusive, and few slaves (especially males) lived long enough to reproduce. The racially tinged conflicts that have marked Haitian history can be traced similarly to slavery," a Library of Congress country study reports.[11]

Despite having expelled French colonial powers during a rebellion led by the formerly enslaved and proclaiming itself the first free Black republic in the West in 1804, Haiti has been unable to release itself from its legacy of slavery and violence. Black/mulatto conflict and human rights abuses are indeed common occurrences in the Haiti of today, which is 95% Afrodescendant.

The Dominican Republic provides us with a different take on Afrodescendants, in pointing out what the realities of life can be for those who choose to deny their slave heritage because of the perceived shame associated with it. Though the Dominican Republic and Haiti share the island of Hispanola—with the D.R. occupying over two-thirds of the island—the two nations are very different culturally, as well as economically. The D.R. maintains a Spanish-centered culture, and because of cultural differences refused to stay under Haiti's rule after the Haitian Revolution occurred. The Dominican Republic emerged as a separate nation from Haiti in 1844 after many years of conflict, submitted to Spanish rule in 1861, then claimed final independence from colonial rule in 1865.

Eighty-four percent of Dominicans have African slave ancestry, though 73% of them selfidentify as 'mulatto'.12 These distinctions allow Dominicans to move more freely though society, while at the same time giving them an upper hand and feeling of superiority over Haitians, who are to this day exploited and abused as sugar laborers in the Dominican Republic. Choosing assimilation into the Western world over embracing its African heritage has proven a beneficial choice for this nation, which now claims one of the fastest growing economies in the Western Hemisphere.

Ada Ferrer, in her book Insurrgent Cuba: Race, Nation and Revolution, 1868-1898, states that in 1846, 36 % of the Cuban population were enslaved. Ferrer claims that more than 595,000 African slaves arrived on the island's shores during the last fifty years of the trade, which ended in 1886. Most of those enslaved worked on Cuba's sugar plantations. Today, an estimated 62% of the nation's 11,346,670 Cubans are of African ancestry. 13Afrodescendants in Cuba continue to face discrimination, despite Castro's revolution, and the Cuban government's attempts at wiping out discriminatory practices. Large numbers of Afro-Cubans have fled Cuba for the United States over the years seeking economic refuge, as Greenbaum notes in her work; she states that for most Afro-Cuban patriots, the vision of social justice in the new republic remained elusive.14

In Bermuda, Jamaica, the Bahamas, Antigua and many other Caribbean nations, the history, circumstances and quality of life for Afrodescendants are similar, if not virtually identical. The bulk of scholarship done in this area verifies this assertion.

A/HRC/Sub.1/58/AC.5/CRP.1
page 7

Percentages of Afrodescendants

Brazil 45% or 83,750,757
United States 13% or 38,445,437
Columbia 26% or 11,168,112
Haiti 95% or 7,715,540
Dom. Rep. 84% or 7,518,028
Cuba 62% or 7,034,935
Jamaica 98% or 2,677,195
Venezuela 10% or 2,537,528

Panama 77% or 2,332,445
Peru 5% or 1,396,281
Ecuador 10% or 1,336,359
Honduras 7.7% or 1,128,449
Canada 2% or 662,200
Bolivia 4% or 354,814
Guyana 45% or 344,377
Puerto Rico 8% or 313,330
The Bahamas 85% or 256,521
Suriname 41% or 179,639
Uruguay 4% or 136,636
French Guiana 66% or 129,033
Belize 31% or 86,631
Costa Rica 2% or 80,323
Nicaragua 13% or 71,046
Guatemala No Records
El Salvador No Records
Mexico No Records
Paraguay No Records
Chile No Records
Argentina No Records15

Total: 169,655,616

Using the American Development Bank estimate of 150 million Afrodescendants in Latin America, the total becomes nearly 190 million. It is evident that studies and further research must be done in order to determine a more accurate population number for Afrodescendants.

Economic Dependence and Poverty

Perhaps the most pervasive and long-lasting effect of the Trans-Atlantic slave trade is the economic dependence that has been forced upon Afrodescendants in its wake. This dependency has affected both Afrodescendants and those residing on the continent of Africa, though in very different ways. In 1441, Portuguese traders returned to Portugal with the first shipment of captive Blacks, setting off a chain of destructive and exploitative events that scholar Robert July claims can never be undone.16 The trade of salt, spices, cloth, firearms, tobacco, spirits, gold and slaves set the stage

for the first instance of African dependency on Europe and, later, on colonial nations. For the continent, this trade—which robbed Africa of many of its greatest artisans, architects and agricultural minds—has had a long-lasting effect on both economy and development, leaving her nations vulnerable to the processes and inequalities of both colonization and neo-colonization.

According to one estimate, 12 million Africans were taken to the Western world as slaves during the Trans-Atlantic slave trade.17 Those enslaved found themselves completely dependent upon their captors for survival; meals, clothing and shelter were provided to the enslaved by the very ones who held them prisoner.

Institutionalized slavery meant that dependence on European powers became a total and complete reality, and it is one that has underscored the lives of Afrodescendants since slavery began in the Western Hemisphere. During the approximately 400-year duration of the TransAtlantic slave trade, this sense of depending on white authorities for individual and collective needs became an ingrained, given part of life, erasing in the minds of most Afrodescendants the memory of a world where Africans once controlled their own destinies.

Constant degradation and the need for bowing and scraping to one's master to get material needs met became a regular way of life for Afrodescendants, who were forced to deny their own humanity in order to survive.

When U.S. and Latin American countries released their enslaved populations from slavery, little to no provisions were made for those newly freed. After centuries of demanding subservience and utter dependence, these nations released multitudes of uneducated, illiterate freed slaves into a reality rife with poverty, unemployment, homelessness and state-sponsored welfare.

Being spewed out of a position of dependence into one of abject poverty, these freed slaves struggled to find respite, to establish their own communities and a sense of political autonomy, and to create a way for themselves to survive despite the odds instituted against them. Churches and schools were hopefully raised by the same hands that had once established the infrastructures of various nations, this time for self-benefit. However, a lack of available resources—land, building materials and access to education among them—meant that the quality of such work was far less than what was necessary for true sustainability within Afrodescendant communities.

Northern America

The City of New Orleans in Louisiana (U.S.) provides a perfect example of Afrodescendant reality in the U.S. Once the largest slave port in the nation and as of August 2005, 67% Afrodescendant, New Orleans is a historically Black and poor city, albeit one with a rich cultural heritage. During the final days of August, a levy break in the city's Lower Ninth Ward followed closely behind Hurricane Katrina, leaving thousands of Afrodescendants trapped in rising waters, without transportation, food, water, electricity or help. Too poor to escape during a mandatory evacuation, Black New Orleanians found themselves suspended on rooftops, and piled on top of one another in the Superdome and Convention Center, calling out to U.S. National Guardsmen— or any passer-by—for help. In most cases, their pleas were ignored. Through television, prior to Hurricane Katrina, the world had seen Black people in the U.S. as powerful and rich. That false image changed when the snapshot taken by Katrina on New

Orleans, showed reality to the world; the majority of Blacks in the U.S. live in "3rd World" conditions, the same as all other Afrodescendants.

Invisibility is a factor of life for many Afrodescendants in the United States, especially when issues of poverty and wealth distribution arise. The Lower Ninth Ward, where the bulk of the damage to New Orleans occurred, is 98.3% Afrodescendant. Thirty-six percent of the Ninth Ward's residents lived in poverty prior to the flooding, and 65% of the families there were headed by single women.18 This poverty has come to mean unspeakable suffering for its victims; after the flood, the National Center for Missing and Exploited Children received over 4,724 reports of missing or "found" children from New Orleans and surrounding areas.

According to the National Urban League, the overall economic status of Afrodescendants in the U.S. measures 57% of their White counterparts.19 Perhaps a more powerful statistic, though, is one offered up by the New York Times, which cites nearly half of all Black men between the ages of 16-64 as being unemployed.

In Canada, incidents of racism and discrimination against Afrodescendants are prevalent and well documented throughout the cities in which they reside, and the economic and social legacies of slavery are becoming increasingly apparent to scholars. Consider what Das Gupta has to say on the subject, in her paper entitled Racism and Paid Work: "Racism continues today as part of our everyday culture, and as a convenient ideology for maintaining cheap labour provided by people of colour and Black people. The ideology of racism has, in post-slavery and post-colonial days, still resulted in the over-representation of Black workers and workers of colour in the least desirable, least secure, poorest paid segments of the workforce. Simultaneously, they have been excluded from better paid, secure, more desirable jobs through systemic practices in the labour market . . .The labour of people of colour and of Black people is assumed to be "natural", "unskilled", and therefore inferior.[20]

Afrodescendants have a long history of residing in Canada, yet still their employment rates lag behind other races, even those who have newly immigrated to the nation. Black unemployment in Canada teeters near 40%, while among European groups the rates are lower than six percent. The 1991 Canadian Census estimates that 31.5% of African-Canadians live below the poverty line compared to 15.7% of the overall Canadian population. When child poverty statistics and the number of single-parent families living below the poverty level in Canada—40% and 23.8% respectively—are figured into the equation, the circumstances of Afro-Canadians become eerily similar to those of group members in the U.S. and abroad. Still another consideration in the poverty equation for Afrodescendants, in both Canada and the U.S., is the violence committed by and against young Black men, high numbers of whom end up dead, incapacitated or incarcerated, thus depriving Afrodescendant families of a primary income earner.

Latin America

The poverty of Afrodescendants in Latin America is staggering, even in a region where being poor is a fact of everyday life for most. The Inter-American Development Bank, in a 1996 study of Afrodescendant quality of life in Argentina, Colombia, Costa Rica, Ecuador, Honduras, Peru, Uruguay and Venezuela, found that Afrodescendant qualities of life in Latin America were much the same in all countries examined.

A/HRC/Sub.1/58/AC.5/CRP.1
page 10

Presently there is little available data regarding the economic status of Afrodescendants in Mexico. Though this deficiency in the research is regrettable, it speaks clearly about the marginalization and near-invisibility of Mexico's Afrodescendant population, and about the failure of the Mexican government to identify the needs and circumstances of its minority groups.

Studies show that over 90% of Afrodescendants in Central and South America live below the poverty line, while working poor paying jobs and receiving limited education. Blacks in Latin America often face race-based discrimination, and they remain the most excluded sector of the population, according to Quince Duncan of the International Scientific Committee of the Slave Route Project In Latin-America. Duncan adds that "the situation of blacks has received less attention than that of indigenous people," and indeed several studies show that Afrodescendants have not been afforded the same protections and development assistance as have indigenous groups.

"Indians and blacks often compete for the same jobs," says Oswaldo Bilbao, executive director of the Center for Ethnic Development in Peru. "Indians say, 'We came first. We're owners of the land.' Blacks say 'I didn't want to come here. But I'm here, and I'm Peruvian.'"

A brief glance at statistics from around the region serves as an eye-opener for those who might question whether Afrodescendants suffer from greater degrees of poverty than other minorities. In Ecuador, 81% of Afrodescendants live below the poverty line. Over fifty percent of Afrodescendants in Brazil live in houses without adequate sanitation, while only 28% of white Brazilians do. Similarly, ninety-eight percent of Black Colombian communities lack basic public utilities.21 El Choco, Colombia, the region on the Pacific Coast where many Afro-Colombians reside, is one of the poorest, most isolated regions in the country; civil warfare between government and guerilla forces has disproportionately affected Afro-Colombians, leaving hundreds of thousands displaced.

Over 80% of all Afrodescendant families in Colombia are poor, with an annual income of around $500US, as opposed to $1,700US for non-Black Colombians.22 Afro-Colombians, like many other groups of Afrodescendants, live in areas where poverty, violence and social unrest run rampant.

Most Afrodescendants in Latin America are relegated to stereotyped jobs, many of them having basis in slavery. Minority Rights Group notes that Black males are often shifted toward lowpaying jobs that require strength and little intellect while women are hired mostly as maids or child care-providers. Many of these women are single mothers with no job security or health insurance provided to them by employers. Garifunas—or the descendants of escaped African slaves—in Guatemala and Honduras also lag behind in quality of life measurement, despite having received some attention from NGOs and aid programs, unlike most other group members. Overall, development programs across the board fail to address Afrodescendant issues. In many cases, major decisions are made regarding historically significant and impoverished communities without Afrodescendant input or involvement, in a continuation of the invisibility that has historically attempted to define their existence.

Caribbean

The World Bank estimates that only 38% of Haitians have access to safe drinking water. Facing wide-spread poverty, gut-wrenching desolation and deforestation and an unemployment rate of 60%, Haiti was virtually abandoned by the Western world after its revolution, perhaps because of its status as a free, Black, formerly enslaved republic with obvious military might in a world where white supremacy has systematically reigned dominant. Haiti remains isolated economically, aside from small amounts of international aid and loans from international banks, and must import 100% of its food from abroad. Haiti's population growth has begun to spin out of control; its overall population is expected to double by 2050[23] despite its standing as the poorest nation in the Western Hemisphere.

Jamaica's yearly income averages $2,690US, and 45% of Jamaican families are headed by single mothers. Unemployment rates average 9.5% for males and 21.8% for females; among youth ages 15-29 unemployment in Jamaica ranged from 20% to 31% nationwide.24 In the city of Kingston, half of all households lack piped water and 60% their own sanitary facilities.

Reuters, in a 1991 study, notes that even though Bermuda has achieved one of the highest per capita incomes in the world, most Afrodescendants have not shared in the prosperity. The study found that black Bermudans with a university degree earned less than white Bermudans who had not even finished high school. In Cuba, where Afrodescendants comprise some 60% of the population, racism has worsened in the past ten years, according to a study conducted by the Cuban government. In Colombia, the National Planning Department acknowledges that 80% of Afro-Colombians live below the poverty line.

Cultural Assault & Discrimination

Slavery in the Americas brought about the cruelest assault imaginable upon a people. The African captives, newly arrived in the Americas, were separated from others who spoke their language and were "seasoned" by violence and degradation. The intent of this "seasoning" was to bring about a slave mentality, destroy the essence of a people, and make them devoid of memory of self. A mental and spiritual "death" did occur, as the enslaved Africans were by brute force assimilated into the dominant, in most cases Euro-centric, culture. Today's Afrodescendants are demonstrating an ever-increasing desire to know and be themselves, and determine their own destiny as a people. This desire translates as a force for ethnogenesis and reparations.

Despite their growing desire for self knowledge and self determination, and despite their shared background and their commonality of experience throughout the world, Afrodescendants from various countries are still deeply divided by nationality, skin color, educational attainment and economic status. Implemented during slavery, the divide and conquer technique used by former colonial masters has so far kept Afrodescendants from coming together as a people in a mass movement whose primary goal would be to improve upon their collective circumstances.

Northern America

In the U.S., government initiatives have boldly sought to destroy Afrodescendant attempts at establishing community, a sustainable culture, political autonomy and even mainstream political

involvement. The intricacies of COINTELPRO—a Federal Bureau of Investigation project that has historically targeted Black leaders—have begun to come to light in recent years, attracting the attention of members of Congress as well as that of social and human rights activists. The American media remains silent on this issue, as it has remained silent on most of the issues affecting Afrodescendants lives. This may be because of a shortage of Afrodescendant reporters and editors within the U.S. media industry, or due to a willful attempt on the part of white society within the United States to make the Afrodescendant invisible and thus irrelevant.

Disenfranchisement has historically been part of the effort to keep Afrodescendants out of the mainstream. In the 2000

U.S. presidential elections, Afrodescendant voters in Florida complained of experiencing intimidation at the polls and of political disenfranchisement, though their concerns fell on deaf ears. Hate crimes against Blacks in the U.S. continue unabated; this was most recently witnessed by the beating of a 64 year-old resident of New Orleans by several white City of New Orleans police officers during the month of October, 2005.

The Center for Democratic Renewal estimates in its 1997 publication They Don't All Wear Sheets: A Chronology of Racist and Far-Right Violence – 1980-1986 that the White Supremacist movement in America consists of 15,000-20,000 activists and another 150,000 people who attend "Christian Patriot" meetings and Ku Klux Klan rallies. Whether white police who beat black civilians are members of this movement or not, such behavior reflects a betrayal of and neglect towards officers' assumed roles of protector and civil servant, and illustrates a deepseated sense of institutional racism that continues to envelop most American bureaucratic institutions today.

The Tulsa, Oklahoma race riot of 1921 is another example of American society at its worse. Sparked by the supposed sexual assault of a white woman by a young black man, white Tulsa residents went on a twenty-four-hour rampage, which resulted in the death of nearly 250 people and the burning of more than 1,000 black homes and businesses. A similar situation occurred in Rosewood, Florida in 1923. These types of incidents have happened frequently throughout American history and continue to take place in the present, as is illustrated in the abandonment and degradation of Black New Orleanians following the breaching of the city's levy.

Instances of hate and neglect are not the only forms of cultural assault and discrimination that Afrodescendants in the United States must face. There exists a severe shortage of media coverage surrounding the daily lives of Afrodescendants, except when criminal conduct is alleged. Harmful stereotypes of Blacks continue to be perpetuated by the U.S. television, film and record industries, while racial epithets and assumptions pertaining to one's blackness are a regular occurrence in most Afrodescendants daily lives. Once again, New Orleans provides a memorable illustration; reports of Black gangs murdering and raping in the dark of night, at the New Orleans Superdome, were beamed around the world by television reporters until, eventually, the stories were revealed as lies and commentators were forced to confess that there was no evidence of marauding gangs terrorizing anyone, or that they even existed

There is considerably less information available with regards to discrimination and cultural assault towards Afrodescendants in Canada than there is in the United States. In a 1995 report prepared for the Municipality of Metropolitan Toronto entitled Hate: Communities Can Respond, it is noted that, according to Metro Toronto Police statistics, racial minorities comprise

the most significant number of individuals violently attacked in hate crimes (54%) and that "black individuals were victimized in more than half (51%) of the racial incidents in 1995."[25]

Latin America

Mexico is only beginning to become aware of its race problem, which has come to the forefront recently. In May of 2005, the Mexican government took heat from American Blacks who criticized the release of a postage stamp featuring 1940's cartoon character Memin Pinguin. The figure bears features that have stereotyped Afrodescendants in the West since the early 19th century, among them over-exaggerated lips and protruded eyes. This image of Blacks is put forth by the mass media of various nations, albeit in different forms, and contributes to the stereotyping and exclusion of Afrodescendants. It is this type of thinking that adds to the burdens Afrodescendants must carry.

Afrodescendants in Latin America face outright race-based discrimination, and it colors nearly every aspect of their daily lives. Wade states that Blacks in Latin America are formally excluded from certain clubs and hotels, subjected to employment ads that call for a good, or "lightskinned" appearance, are insulted in the streets, harassed by citizens and targeted by police.26

These realities are in direct contradiction to the theory of racial democracy that exists in Latin America; this philosophy argues that being black is a transitory state which can be altered by whitening through miscegenation or wealth accumulation.27 In both Brazil and Colombia, the countries with the largest Afro-Latino populations in South America, Afrodescendants are and always have been among the poorest, least educated and lowest paid citizens. Data debunks the racial democracy theory and illustrates a definite connection between discrimination and poverty in Latin America.

Not least among the forms of cultural assault and discrimination directed at Afrodescendants are the human rights abuses that have occurred over time and that continue to occur: forced assimilation and breeding, loss of mother tongue and indigenous religion, a disconnect from family history, genealogy and African nation of origin, along with an exploitation of Black culture by the popular media are among these. Because of such practices, there exists a resulting sense of shame for many that stems from being of African slave ancestry; it is often enough to keep Afrodescendants from identifying as such.

Caribbean

The U.S. Department of State reported in 2004 that though slavery was abolished in the British Empire in 1834, racial segregation continued to be practiced in Bermuda's schools, restaurants, hotels, and other public places until the 1960s. Although racial discrimination in any form is not legally tolerated in today's multiracial Bermudian society, the State Department claims that race issues continue to play a role in Bermuda both politically and socially.

In Cuba, interracial relationships are widely frowned upon. Afro-Cubans are often regarded as more prone to criminal behavior, and Eurocentric standards of beauty dominate the culture. Despite attempts by the government to eliminate racism from Cuban society, racist ideas and attitudes continue to persist. Likewise, Jorge Ramirez of the Black Association for the Defense

and Advancement of Human Rights says "the racism in Cuba is not in the laws. It's in the mentality of people."

Education

Northern America

Within the U.S., the Urban League has found that teachers with less than three years experience teach in minority schools at twice the rate that they teach in white schools. This has a direct effect on the quality of education that group members receive and their level of educational attainment. While preschool enrollment for blacks dropped three points from 60% in 2004, white preschool enrollment increased four percent; these gradually declining numbers, for the most part, are indicative of the educational status of blacks throughout the nation.

At present, one in five Afro-Canadians are either attending university or have earned a bachelors degree. Perhaps the most notable compliant regarding the state of public education for youth in Canada is the lack of a presence of Afro-Canadian history; the Ministry of State – Multiculturalism is currently working to address this issue.

Latin America

Afrodescendants in Latin-America receive little education, if any at all. In Brazil, the illiteracy rate for blacks over 15 is 20%, while only 8% for whites. The U.S.-based Chronicle of Higher Education states that "While 45 percent of the country's 170 million people defined themselves as either black or pardo—mixed race—in the 2000 census, only 17 percent of university graduates are of mixed race and only 2% are black."28 Black Brazilians average 6.4 years of schooling.29 Similarly, Afro-Colombian communities struggle with an illiteracy rate of 32%, and with a scenario in which a mere 38% of Afrodescendant teenagers can attend secondary school. Only 2% of Afro-Colombian youth attend university.

Caribbean

In nearly all of the above-listed communities and in the Caribbean, Afrodescendants are not afforded the same educational opportunities as members of other groups. These discrepancies are most blatantly visible when comparing the gaps that exist between white and black levels of educational attainment. On the whole, Afrodescendants represent a disproportionate number of high school drop-outs in their individual nations. Many of them are unable to read or write.

Additionally, their own group history—in all nations—is left out of virtually all state-based school curriculums. This shows a blatant disregard for the true historical record of each nation, particularly with regard to their own slavery past. The United Nations is attempting to address this issue with its Trans Atlantic Slave Trade Program, which seeks to incorporate information about the slave trade into school curriculums. In most nations, though, this program has yet to be implemented; if adopted, it could prove detrimental to national interests in its highlighting of the exploitation of Blacks and states' complicity in this matter.

Poverty and a lack of educational resources often translate into inadequate education for children in Cuba. TransAfrica notes that the Abel Santa Maria School, which educates visually impaired children, has one functional computer for 212 children.30 Cuba has a high literacy rate of 96%, though only 81% of its citizens enroll in secondary school, and a mere 13% attend college. Ninety-three percent of Haiti's population is illiterate—a staggering number—while in Jamaica, government cutbacks have meant less access to education for many.

Health Care

Northern America

The health of Afrodescendants in the U.S. continues to decline. Infant mortality rates are twice as high for blacks, and adults experience disproportionately high mortality rates from causes that include heart disease and stroke, homicide, accidents, cancer, cirrhosis and diabetes. Afrodescendant males suffer from heart disease at twice the rate of whites, and blacks are more likely to die from breast cancer and prostate cancer.31

The Urban League, in its 2005 report, states that HIV infects Afrodescendants at a rate five times that of whites, that black women are twenty times more likely to become infected than white women and that blacks are five times more likely to be the victims of a homicide. A report issued by the U.S. Commission on Civil Rights admits that discrimination in healthcare is a reality for blacks in the United States.

Some scholars believe that many of the mental health issues affecting Afrodescendant communities can be traced back to their slave ancestry, or at least attributed to the trauma suffered by some in the wake of that legacy. Harvard psychiatrist Dr. Chester Price describes the environment in which American Blacks live as a mundane extreme environment, or an environment in which racism and subtle oppression are constant, continuing and mundane. The "microaggressions" which Afrodescendants suffer, Price claims, have had a harsh impact on the psyche and worldview of Blacks. These injuries can affect Blacks' sense of self-perception and behavior, and are stressful, detracting and energy-consuming.32

Further research is required regarding the state of health for Afrodescendants in Canada.

Latin America

Health in Latin America is a major concern for all communities, but Afrodescendants find themselves both unhealthier and with less access to care than other groups. At present, no available data specific to Afrodescendants regarding health in Mexico has been located. Further research is required. Minority Rights Group notes that health insurance in Colombia is afforded to only 10% of Afrodescendant communities, versus 40% of white communities.33 In Brazil—a country with a 62 in 1,000 black infant mortality rate—the white population is 2.5 times healthier than the Afrodescendant population. Guyana's Afrodescendants struggle with the rising spread of AIDS; it is a disease that continues to affect them disproportionately, and which results in lower life expectancy, higher infant mortality and death rates, as well as lower population and growth rates. In the Esmeraldas region of Ecuador, Afrodescendants have a higher rate of both suicide and homicide, while the Garifuna in Honduras' coastal region show much higher HIV/AIDS rates than do the general population.

Across Latin America, statistics show that Afrodescendants overall experience higher HIV/AIDS rates, a severe shortage of doctors, higher infant mortality rates, lower life expectancy and higher incidences of diabetes, cancer, hypertension, high blood pressure and respiratory disease.

Caribbean

The Caribbean is no exception when examining issues of health and inadequacies in health care. Haiti has a mere life expectancy of 54 years and an infant mortality rate of 71 per 1000. The World Bank estimates that malnutrition affects half of all children in Haiti, and that eleven HIV positive babies are born in Haiti every day. Overall, 300,000 people in this Caribbean nation are HIV positive, and Haiti and the Dominican Republic account for 85% of the reported HIV/AIDS cases in the Caribbean. Jamaica has a higher life expectancy rate, at 75.7 years on average, but many Jamaicans suffer from respiratory disease and high rates of diabetes. A 1997 report by the American Association of World Health reports that the U.S. embargo against Cuba has resulted in a significant rise in suffering and deaths in Cuba, where life expectancy averages 76 years. Cuba's infant mortality rate is 7% for the general Cuban population; specific statistics for AfroCubans were not found.

Legal Right to Equality Before the Law

It is out of the legacy of slavery that conflict between Afrodescendants and Western political and legal systems was born. Afrodescendants in the Western Hemisphere have historically been disenfranchised, targeted by law enforcement officials and denied recourse for injuries sustained at the hands of racist systems. After centuries of being denied legal equality before the law, and after generations of suffering beneath the weight of legal, economic and social oppression, many Afrodescendants have become apathetic and separatist in their leanings. Efforts at recompense to Afrodescendant communities for abuses and injuries suffered have been on the whole largely non-existent, and even when attempted are usually ineffective because of mistrust of the system, and due to cloudy intentions and protected interests on the part of various states.

Yet the most damaging inequality before the law may be with regard to international law that protects the right of minorities to enjoy their original culture, to profess and practice their original religion, and to use their original language. While other minorities are able to enjoy the protections offered in Article 27 of the International Covenant on Civil and Political Rights, and the Declaration on the Rights of Minorities, Afrodescendants do not have equal protection under these laws, as their original language, culture and religion were taken from them by force during slavery and are denied to them in the lingering effects of slavery.

Northern America

Haney and Zimbardo write that "At the start of the 1990s, the U.S. had more black men (between the ages of 20 and 29) under the control of the nation's criminal justice system than the total number in college. This and other factors have led some scholars to conclude that, crime control policies are a major contributor to the disruption of the family, the prevalence of single parent families, the number of children being raised without a father in the ghetto, and the inability of people to get the jobs still available."[34]

Race-based discrimination affects nearly every portion of the justice system in the United States, and while Afrodescendants comprise approximately 13% of the total U.S. population, they make up over 80% of inmates imprisoned. These numbers make it easy to conclude that disparities do indeed exist, and that Afrodescendants are therefore not entitled to legal equality before the law.

A/HRC/Sub.1/58/AC.5/CRP.1
page 17

In the U.S., Amnesty International reports that evidence of racial discrimination and ill treatment and bias by police has been widely documented. Abuses include racist language, harassment, unjustified stops and searches and arbitrary arrests, as well as racial disparities in death penalty rates and incarceration. Amnesty states that police and prison guards frequently abuse prisoners with racist statements such as "nigger, boy, porch monkey and coon," and exhibit an excessive use of force, electro shock and tasering.35 In addition, there are numerous instances throughout U.S. history of Afrodescendants being targeted and even killed by police. In Chicago, of 115 civilians shot dead by police between 1990-98, 82 were black. The Sentencing Project states that an estimated one in ten Black males in America are incarcerated; if Black males in county and local jails are included in this estimate, the number rises to one in every seven. This is in stark contrast to the 1% of White males overall who are presently incarcerated in the U.S.36 These disparities begin in the courtroom: the Urban League notes that Afrodescendants receive on average sentences that are six months longer than those of whites; Blacks are also more frequently sentenced to death for alleged crimes. These numbers have had an enormous impact on relations between Afrodescendant communities and law enforcement officials, as is noted by former U.S. Attorney General Janet Reno in the following statement in 1999: "For too many people, especially in minority communities, the trust that is so essential to effective policing does not exist because residents believe that police have used excessive force, that law enforcement is too aggressive, that law enforcement is biased, disrespectful, and unfair."

In Canada, in the 1990's, a major study was conducted by the Commission on Systemic Racism in the Ontario Criminal Justice System concerning the impact of racism on Afrodescendant communities in Ontario. This commission was organized in response to the deterioration of the relationship between the Ontario Police Department and Afrodescendants in Ontario. "Blacks are over-represented in the prison population," the study found. "In the six year period leading up to 1993, it was found that the Black population of Ontario increased by 36% while the number of Black prisoners admitted to Ontario prisons increased by 204%.37

Latin America

Disparities in sentencing and incarceration rates for Afrodescendants are present in Latin America as well. A State Department Human Rights Report for 2003 found that "discrimination against blacks and indigenous people continued unabated, and that "people of color were five times more likely to be shot or killed in the course of a law enforcement action than were persons perceived to be white."

Amnesty further notes that Afro-Brazilians are disproportionately targeted by security forces and are routinely denied the advantages allowed to white middle-class criminal suspects. In 2000, Sao Paulo reported that in 1999 54% of criminal suspects killed in the area by police were Black. Experts have testified that of those detained in Brazil, the majority are Afro-Brazilian. A disproportionate number of

Afrodescendants are also held in jails and prisons in Colombia and Guatemala.

Caribbean

Bermuda is known internationally as a country with one of the highest per capita incomes in the world and is also known as a world leader in imprisonment. Ninety-eight percent of Bermuda's inmates are black, and that means 148 out of every 10,000 black males in Bermuda is in prison.

Disparities in sentencing and imprisonment in most Caribbean nations are difficult to prove at this point in the research.

Land and Home Ownership

Northern America

Fewer than 50% of black families own their own homes in the U.S, versus over 70% of whites, according to The Urban League. The League claims that Blacks are denied mortgages and home improvement loans at twice the rate of whites, and there are many instances of land being taken from Afrodescendants. In Louisiana, the Orleans Parish Levy Board has been ordered by the Superior Court of Louisiana to reimburse Afrodescendants for land the agency pushed them from. In 2001, the Associated Press compiled a series of articles entitled Torn From The Land, which documented similar takings. The AP documented 107 incidents of land-takings, in which 406 Black landowners lost more than 24,000 acres of farmland, along with 85 smaller properties.

Further research is required in determining Afrodescendant land rights and home ownership rates in Canada.

Latin America

Afrodescendants in Latin America are becoming increasingly involved in disputes over ancestral lands. Minority Rights Group argues that the lands on which Afrodescendants reside are often targeted for taking by developers and corporate investors because of a failure to recognize Afrodescendants as the rightful owners of land. Government authorities, MRG adds, often neglect to protect local populations from predatory companies and entrepreneurs. "Companies are allowed virtually unrestricted access into Afrodescendant areas in search of natural resources, while also encouraging colonization of traditionally Afrodescendant lands," the NGO states, in its publication Afrodescendants, Discrimination and Economic Exclusion in Latin-America.

In Brazil, over 2000 Quilombos, or Afrodescendants, occupy some 30,000 hectares of land. Thus far, only 70 of 743 have had their lands titled. In Afrodescendant owned areas, especially in the rainforests of respective nations, development threatens to destroy the ecological order of things. Still—and despite the fact that large tracts of land have historically meant refuge from slavery and exclusion—developers seek to capitalize on tourism growth, and obtaining land titles for ancestral lands is becoming increasingly difficult.

Caribbean

Further research is necessary in determining land rights and home ownership rates for countries in the Caribbean.

Summary

This paper, at this point in time, is a limited attempt at providing interested parties with an overview of the quality of life issues that face Afrodescendants in the Americas Region; it is in no way comprehensive, but instead, is a work continuously in progress. Allowances must be made by the reader for time constraints, limited available scholarship and data in certain areas and for the fact that this work is the first of its kind in seeking to assess the situation of

Afrodescendants as a whole in various countries. Existing scholarship is country-specific; this work seeks to be group specific, and to be all-encompassing.

Nevertheless, it can be stated unequivocally that Afrodescendants throughout the region are subjected to similar forms of oppression, economic exclusion and discrimination. This similarity of experience is one of the things that defines them as a group; they are—for the most part— minorities in their countries of residence and are treated as having less importance than the majority population. Little can be done to alter their respective circumstances without changes in state-sponsored policy, greater economic inclusion and recompense for injuries and human rights abuses suffered. These things cannot occur without changing of societal mindsets with regard the lingering effects of slavery in the Americas. Until these tasks are undertaken by countries and international bodies as well, Afrodescendants will continue to face a decline in the quality of their lives.

Reparations as a Remedy

International law supports reparations a bona fide remedy. The compensation for internment of Japanese Americans in the U.S. during World War II, the apology and compensation of the Governor of Puerto Rico for the domestic surveillance of its citizens in the late 1940s, the German government's various compensation programs following World War II, and New Zealand's reparations paid for theft of Maori land by the British during the late 1800s all support the idea of reparations as a remedy.

Detractors of reparations— both black and white — trivialize their importance and say that it "reinforces the notion of victimhood" despite the fact that the United Nations and other international bodies contradict this false notion. It is interesting to note how the use of the term "victim" can be distorted in a way that implies helplessness, dependency and weakness. In fact the opposite is true. Rosa Parks was a "victim" of racism, but her bravery ignited the modern civil rights movement. Jews were "victims" of the Holocaust, but it did not prevent them from successfully suing for reparations in a variety of courts. The Cherokee, Choctaw and Lakota were "victims" of genocide yet they have been successful in receiving compensation for the genocidal behavior of the United States toward them. In none of these instances were the "victims" helpless and in all of them, there is an eye toward seeking long-denied justice for their people. So it is with the unpaid debt to the stolen people from Africa.

It is recommended that as a preliminary step in reparations, each of the integral states wherein Afrodescendants reside exempt them from payment of taxes. If the states find that tax exemption is not possible, it is recommended that the entire tax revenue from Afrodescendants be invested back into their communities by the current federal, state and local authorities until such time as Afrodescendants are able to collect and handle their own tax revenues. It is further recommended that the United Nations create a permanent forum for Afrodescendants, similar to the forum created for the Indigenous Peoples. Since Afrodescendants are a stateless people, they have only the UN to look to for protection. Within a forum, Afrodescendant leaders can peacefully meet together for the purpose of collective decision making. Most importantly, under a UN forum, Afrodescendants will be assured of receiving expert guidance, which is vital to their continued rise and development as a human family.

A/HRC/Sub.1/58/AC.5/CRP.1
page 20

---

1 Should America Pay?, Slave Taxes

2. The Trans-Atlantic Slave Trade, a Database on CD-ROM, Eltis, Behrendt, Richardson and Klein, Cambridge University Press, 1999

3. Africans in America Pt.1, Public Broadcasting System (PBS) Web Site, Oct.12, 2005

4. The Negro Holocaust: Lynching and Race riots in the United States, 1880-1950, Gibson, Robert, Yale-New Haven Teachers Institute, 1979

5. Intelligence Report, Southern Poverty Law Center Web Site, Oct. 12, 2005

6. Early Black Canadian History. Fabbi, 2003

8. Blacks in Mexico. Vinson, B. 2000. Library of Congress Web Site, Sept. 26, 2005

9. Mexico Slow to Confront Racial Issues, Samuels, L., Dallas Morning News Web Site 2005

10. The Region: Race, Latin-America's Invisible Challenge, Inter-American Development Bank, January, 1997

11. Haiti: A Country Study, Library of Congress Web Site, Oct. 13, 2005

12. Dominican Republic: A Country Study, Library of Congress, Web Site, Oct. 13, 2005

13. World Fact Book, CIA Web Site, Oct. 13, 2005

14. Afro-Cubans in Exile: Tampa, Florida, 1886-1984, Greenbaum, Susan, 2002

15. Afrodescendants in Latin America: How Many?, Inter-American Dialogue, 2001

16. Robert July, A History of The African People, Waveland Press, Prospect Heights, Illinois, 1998

17. Johannes Postma, The Atlantic Slave Trade, London, Greenwood Press, 2003

18. Greater New Orleans Community Development Organization Web Site, 2005

19. State of The Black Union Report 2005, National Urban League, 2005

20. Racism and Paid Work, Tania Das Gupta, Garamond Press, Toronto, 1996, at 1-40, esp. at pp. 14-15

21. Afrodescendants, Discrimination and Economic Exclusion in Latin-America, Minority Rights Group International, 2005

22. Speech, Murillo, Luis Gilberto, former governor of Choco State, Colombia, U.S., 2001

23. UNICEF, Web Site

24. Regional Core Health Data System Country Profile, Pan American Health Organization 25. African Canadian Legal Clinic, 2002

26. Ethnicity, multiculturalism and social policy in Latin America: Afro-Latin and Indigenous populations, Wade, Peter, 2004

27. Report for Congress, Gibando

28. Long after slavery, inequities remain in Peru, Miami Herald, 2004

29. From Racial Democracy to Affirmative Action: Changing State Policy on Race in Brazil, Latin American Research Review, Vol. 39, No.1, Feb.2004

30. The Consequences of the U.S. Economic Embargo on Afro-Cubans: A Transcript of Proceedings, TransAfrica Forum, 1997

31. Health Resources and Services Administration, Health Care Rx: Access for All, President's Initiative on Race, 1998

32. Mundane Extreme Environmental Stress and African-American Families: A Case for Recognizing Different Realities, Grace Carroll, Journal of Comparative Family Studies, 2005

33. CRS Report for Congress, Afro-Latinos in Latin America and Considerations for U.S. Policy, Claire Ribando, Congressional Research Service, The Library of Congress, 2005

34. Twenty-five Years After the Stanford Prison Experiment. Haney, C. & Zimbardo, P. American Psychologist, Vol. 53, 1998

35. Racism and The Administration of Justice, Amnesty International, 1999

36. New Prison Population Figures, Crisis and Opportunity, The Sentencing Project, July 2002 37 African Canadian Legal Clinic, 2002

Written and Oral Statements to the UN in 2006

Written Statement to the 58th Sub-Commission on the Promotion and Protection of Human Rights, Agenda Item 5 C: prevention of discrimination and Protection of Minorities, August 2006

For well over nine years we have traveled to Geneva. For nine years we have spoken to the Sub-Commission about the Afrodescendant people. We know that we are a nation of people: history, all the wise scientists, and you, in your hearts, will bear witness that we, Afrodescendants, are an ancient people who descended from Abraham. We were scattered through slavery, stripped of our original language, culture and religion, living today, suffering the lingering effects of slavery.

The first time we spoke at the UN, to the Working Group on Minorities, concerning our human rights, they began seeking to find a way for us to fit into the definition of the ICCPR, for we mimic the mother tongue, culture and religion of our slave-masters' children, having been robbed of our own.

The Sub-Commission gave the Working Group on Minorities a wisely worded mandate to consider the "lingering effects of slavery." Over the years the Working Group did consider the lingering effects of slavery and you have the results today. Leaders of Afrodescendants, about 250 million of us, met in La Ceiba, Honduras in 2001, and again in Chincha, Peru in 2005, under the protection of the UN, in the sight of Nations, and affirmed our commitment to one another. This was done in the presence of the Office of the High Commissioner for Human Rights.

We want formal UN recognition of our self-chosen name, Afrodescendants. We want restoration to the human families of the earth. For the sake of simple justice, and to correct a grave error, oh United Nations hear our prayer! In error, the UN granted recognition, restoration and reparations 60 years ago to a scattered people who claimed to be the seed of Abraham, the victims of 400 years of slavery. The result of that grave UN error is ongoing war and terror for the entire world today.

We, Afrodescendants, are the scattered orphan children, descended from 400 years of plantation slavery. Our recognition by the UN would not bring war and terror. It would, instead, correct a grave wrong and bring the truth to a suffering world. It has been our prayer that the Sub-Commission and the Working Group on Minorities would be our symbolic "dry land," allowing us, the slave descendants, to cross our symbolic "red sea."

The good works of the Working Group on Minorities and the Sub-Commission cannot go unnoticed unless the Human Rights Department fails 250 million souls altogether. We call upon the United Nations to do the right thing, for the sake of peace, and for the sake of all Nations of the earth. The pathway of the slave-descendants' collective human rights recognition and restoration must be protected and assured.

Statement to the 12th Session of the Working Group on Minorities, August, 2006

Speaker: Silis Muhammad

Greetings Mr. Chairman, Members of the Working Group on Minorities.

My name is Silis Muhammad. For well over nine years we have traveled to Geneva. For nine years we have spoken to you about the Afrodescendant people. We know that we are a nation of people: history, all the wise scientists, and you, in your hearts, will bear witness that we, Afrodescendants, are an ancient people who descended from Abraham. We were scattered through slavery, stripped of our original language, culture and religion, living today, suffering the lingering effects of slavery.

The first time we spoke at the UN, to the Working Group on Minorities, concerning our human rights, you began seeking to find a way for us to fit into the definition of the ICCPR, for we mimic the mother tongue, culture and religion of our slave-masters' children, having been robbed of our own. The Working Group on Minorities received a wisely worded mandate from the Sub-Commission, to consider the "lingering effects of slavery." Over the years the Working Group did consider the lingering effects of slavery and you have the results today. Leaders of Afrodescendants, about 250 million of us, met in La Ceiba, Honduras in 2001, and again in Chincha, Peru in 2005, under the protection of the UN, in the sight of Nations, and affirmed our commitment to one another. This was done in the presence of the Office of the High Commissioner for Human Rights.

We want formal UN recognition of our self-chosen name, Afrodescendants. We want restoration to the human families of the earth. For the sake of simple justice, and to correct a grave error, O United Nations hear our prayer! In error, the UN granted recognition, restoration and reparations 60 years ago to a scattered people who claimed to be the seed of Abraham, the victims of 400 years of slavery. The result of that grave UN error is ongoing war and terror for the entire world today.

We, Afrodescendants, are the scattered orphan children, descended from 400 years of plantation slavery. Our recognition by the UN would not bring war and terror. It would, instead, correct a grave wrong and bring the truth to a suffering world. It has been our prayer that the Sub-Commission and the Working Group on Minorities would be our symbolic "dry land," allowing us, the slave descendants, to cross our symbolic "red sea."

The good works of the Working Group on Minorities and the Sub-Commission cannot go unnoticed unless the Human Rights Department fails 250 million souls altogether. We call upon the United Nations to do the right thing, for the sake of peace, and for the sake of all Nations of the earth. The pathway of the slave-descendants' collective human rights recognition and restoration must be protected and assured.

Written and Oral Statements to the UN in 2005

Statements delivered in 2005 were heard and responded to by the UN.

Written and Oral Statements to the United Nations in 2005

Table of Contents

1. Oral Statement to the 57th Session of the Sub-Commission on the Promotion and Protection of Human Rights, August 2005

2. Oral Statement to the 11th Session of the Working Group on Minorities, May 2005

3. Oral Statement to the 61st Session of the Commission on Human Rights, April 2005

4. Written Statement to the 61st Session of the Commission on Human Rights, April 2005

Oral Statement to the 57th Sub-Commission on the Promotion and Protection of Human Rights., August 2005, Agenda Item 5C: Prevention of discrimination and protection of minorities

Speaker: Mr. Silis Muhammad

Thank you Mr. Chairman.

Several years ago, I was questioned by a young lady from Europe. She asked, "Isn't it rather naive on your part, for you to come to the house of the same people who enslaved you, seeking justice?" I responded, "I believe that there are people in the UN who know what is right, and I have faith."

The Working Group on Minorities, inquiring into their area of expertise, found there was not a place established within the UN that Afrodescendants could fit, because Afrodescendants are coming back to life absent their mother tongue, original culture and religion. The Working Group on Minorities began seeking to find a way for us.

Under another mandate, following the 2001 Durban World Conference, the UN appointed a Working Group on People of African Descent.

There is a vast difference between Afrodescendants and people of African descent. While we enjoy the same comely color, we both view ourselves as being different. People of African descent still have their original identity: their mother tongue, culture, and religion, while Afrodescendants mimic the mother tongue, culture, and religion of our slavemaster's children. Our identity, our dignity, and thus our essence, was taken. We can put on all the African clothes we want, and we still don't have our identity.

We, collectively, are rendered a stateless people by the depravation of these most precious human rights, as defined by Article 27 of the ICCPR. People of African descent can enjoy the comfort of their tribal kinships and the protection of their governments. We, Afrodescendants, cannot. We have only the UN to look to in the hopes of protection.

The Working Group on Minorities is instrumental in bringing us together – some 250 million souls who have been left out: in existence, yet unobserved by the UN but for the Working Group on Minorities.

The Working Group on Minorities also views us, Afrodescendants, as being different from people of African descent. Is this a contributing reason why the Working Group on Minorities is now under attack?

In La Ceiba, Honduras, in 2002, the Working Group on Minorities orchestrated a seminar in which Afrodescendant leaders from 19 countries chose the term, Afrodescendants, as an identity. Since this date, we have been asking the UN to recognize our self-chosen identity and the Working Group on Minorities has recognized us. Afrodescendants enjoy a permanent place on the agenda of the Working Group on Minorities. Is this a contributing reason why this working group is under attack?

On behalf of Afrodescendants, we recommend that the Working Group on Minorities be given more power, not less. We recommend that our self-chosen identity, Afrodescendants, be recognized by the entire UN, and by the governments under which we live. We further recommend sanctions against all Governments that have deprived us, for every day we have been so denied human rights.

Oral Statement to the 11th Session of the Working Group on Minorities (2005)

Statement of Silis Muhammad, read by Ishmael Abdul-Salaam

Thank you Mr. Chairman.

All For Reparations and Emancipation AFRE is an international NGO in consultative status. We are concerned with the lingering effects of slavery on Afrodescendant minorities throughout the Americas Region and Slavery Diaspora.

We, the Afrodescendants, have been identified by the majority population as sambo, negro, colored, and African American, among other names. We are unlike other people of African descent who live today in different parts of the world. They still have their identity: their mother tongue, culture and religion, and their tribal kinships. They can enjoy the protection and assistance of their national authorities, if they so choose. But we, the Afrodescendants, who are rendered a stateless people by the deprivation of these most precious rights: the enjoyment of our mother tongue, culture and religion, have only the UN to look to in the hope of protection.

When we first encountered the United nations and the Working Group on Minorities we said, "We do not have collective human rights as defined by the UN." The Working Group on Minorities said to us, "We will have to find out where you fit."

Through the years the Working Group on Minorities organized several seminars that culminated in the 2002 seminar in LaCeiba, Honduras. In LaCeiba, on March 24, we chose for ourselves the term Afrodescendants as an identity to be recognized by the UN.

The Working Group on Minorities not only brought us together, it is the vital instrument that helped us to arrive at this identity, Afrodescendants. When we reported that our mother tongue, culture and religion were forcibly taken and we questioned whether or not we had human rights, the Working Group on Minorities responded. This Working Group on Minorities is instrumental in igniting the torch of our definitive identity. For us, the Working Group on Minorities is the soul, if we could use that word, of the UN. It has brought together 250 million souls who otherwise would have been left out: in existence, but unobserved by the UN.

We have pledged this name: Afrodescendants. In doing this we invite the hopes of the protection of the UN. We, the Afrodescendants, appear as a newly born baby and the Working Group on Minorities is our breath of life. Now, if the Working Group on Minorities is shut down, we will not survive. Both the UN, and we, will fall short.

In order to be free to live in dignity, we must have our own destiny. This cannot happen without reparations (otherwise stated, restoration), which begins with the full recognition of the UN and the governments under which we live. Recognition must be followed by compensation for them having deprived us of human rights during the lingering effects of slavery.

Our destiny is intertwined in our diverse governments and it should not be. Afrodescendants have a common destiny and they should be intertwined with each other.

We recommend that the Working Group on Minorities assist us in our efforts to have our self-chosen identity recognized by the entire UN and by the governments under which we live. We want Freedom to live in dignity.

Thank you Mr. Chairman.

Footnote: After the formation of the Universal Declaration of Human Rights, the U.S. Government, in particular, acted against us with knowledge. They accepted a duty to inform us of human rights, and they not only failed to inform us, they set in motion ongoing tactics to prevent our obtaining human rights.

Oral Statement to the 61st Commission on Human Rights (2005) Agenda Item 14 b Minorities

Note: This statement was prepared to be delivered by Mr. Silis Muhammad, but it was not delivered orally due to a schedule change of the CHR. It was delivered to the Members in written form by the Secretariat.

We, the Afrodescendant people, living in the position of minorities throughout the Americas Region and Slavery Diaspora, want to be recognized on the agenda, or in a decision or resolution of the Commission on Human Rights.

We, the formerly so-called African Americans have chosen for ourselves an identity: Afrodescendants.

Leaders of Afrodescendants, from 19 countries, met in the year 2002 in La Ceiba, Honduras, under the supervision of the UN Working Group on Minorities. We have often praised and thanked this Working Group for they, in their wisdom, knew that we had no human rights. They have recognized us and sought diligently to help us. In La Ceiba we chose Afrodescendants as our internal recognized identity, for we have these kinships and uniqueness, to wit: we are a dead, a stateless people, or civilly dead to the knowledge of self: and have been, or are, purposely, being kept so, especially by the United States.

Due to slavery, we are 400 years removed from the land in which we lived, Africa. In the lingering effects of slavery, we are rendered a stateless people.

We are now experiencing ethnogenesis. At present, we Afrodescendants, numbering 250 million, have no collective protective human rights. Since, as a people, we are not recognized as citizens of any country, we call upon member States of the UN to grant us recognition and the protection of the UN.

We wish to do what the Scriptural prodigal son did: get up from the savage condition in which we have been forced to live, through assimilation, and return to our home to be welcomed by our brothers and by our father. The world knows that we originally came from Arabia: all of us. It is the home of civilization and we were there at the origin of civilization.

The doors cannot close upon us, the Afrodescendants. We are an element of the earth, born from the beginnings of civilization, and all people know that of us. We exist. We were scattered through no choice of our own, but through the European slave trade which deemed us savages.

Will the Commission on Human Rights recognize us?

Written Statement to the 61st Session of the Commission on Human Rights (2005), Agenda Item 14: Specific groups and individuals: (b) Minorities

We, the Afrodescendant minorities, formerly the so-called African Americans, throughout the Americas Region and Slavery Diaspora, have been attending and intervening at the Commission on Human Rights for eight years. We have been praying for our most basic human rights: our language, culture, and religion; and, we have been repeatedly asking for the recognition of our self-chosen name, Afrodescendants. The Working Group on Minorities has recognized us, the Afrodescendant minorities, suffering the lingering effects of slavery. We seek the recognition of the entire United Nations.

We are unlike other people of African descent who live today in different parts of the world. They still have their identity: their mother tongue, culture, religion, and their tribal kinships. They can enjoy the protection and assistance of their national authorities, if they so choose. But we, who were rendered a stateless people by slavery, were deprived of all of these most precious rights, and are denied and deprived still of these rights: the right to enjoy our mother tongue, culture and religion. We cannot reclaim our grandparents: DNA testing can only group us with a particular tribe in Africa.

Thus, we are orphans in the earth to this day. Four hundred years of forced mixed breeding during slavery and its lingering effects have rendered us a stateless people, unprotected by human rights law.

Due in part to the efforts of the Working Group on Minorities, for the first time in the history of our sojourn we who are descendants of enslaved Africans collectively took on the identity of Afrodescendants at La Ceiba, Honduras in March, 2002.

The Working Group on Minorities has placed Afrodescendants in their reports and on their agenda as Afrodescendant minorities. We submit this as a working definition of Afrodescendants: peoples who 1) were forcibly dispossessed of their homeland, Africa; 2) were transported to the Americas and Diaspora for the purpose of enslavement; 3) and were subjected to slavery; 4) were subjected to forced mixed breeding and rape; 5) have experienced, through force, the loss of mother tongue, culture and religion; 6) and have experienced racial discrimination due to lost ties or partially lost ties to our original identity.

We have collectively given name to ourselves: Afriodescendants. We are defining ourselves. Will the Commission on Human Rights acknowledge our decisions and use our chosen name in its documents? Will the Commission on Human Rights fix the time when it considers minorities on its agenda as is done with the Indigenous Peoples, out of consideration for our economic condition? Afrodescendant leaders are in a comparable position with the leaders of Indigenous Peoples.

The United Nations is perceived to be the zenith body of law and order in the world. What other body of law can we call upon? We call upon you, the Commission on Human Rights. The Commission on Human Rights has a more respected voice than do we, the minority. As ex-slaves, having experienced civil death and ethnogenesis, what more can we ask, or of whom can we ask that our self-chosen name, Afrodescendants, be used by the Commission on Human Rights, and that the class of persons fitting the description of minority, have a fixed time to speak to the Commission on Human Rights.

We sincerely appreciate the decisions made by the Commission on Human Rights on our behalf, and we respectfully ask the Commission to consider our recommendation: that the Commission on Human Rights use the term Afrodescendants and the the Commission on Human Rights fix the time on their agenda when minority issues will be discussed out of consideration for Afrodescendants, who, as human rights scholars well know, are today among the poorest of the poor.

Written and Oral Statements to the UN in 2004

Statements delivered in 2004 were heard and responded to by the UN.

Written and Oral Statements to the United Nations in 2004

Table of Contents

1. Oral Statement to the 56th Session of the Sub-Commission on the Promotion and Protection of Human Rights, August 2004

2. Written Statement to the 56th Session of the Sub-Commission on the Promotion and Protection of Human Rights, August 2004

3. Oral Statement to the 60th Session of the Commission on Human Rights, April 2004

4. Written Statement to the 60th Session of the Commission on Human Rights, April 2004

5. Oral Statements to the 10th Session of the Working Group on Minorities, March 2004 (three statements)

1) Oral Statement to the Sub-Commission on the Promotion and Protection of Human Rights
Fifth Sixth Session, 26 July to 13 August, 2004
Agenda Item 5 ©) Prevention of discrimination and protection of minorities
Speaker: Mr. Silis Muhammad

We, the Afro descendant minorities, numbering over 250 million souls in the region of the Americas and Slavery Diaspora, do not have collective human rights protection under the United Nations.

We have been bringing our prayers to the Working Group on Minorities for more than eight years. This Working Group, made up of five Sub-Commissioners, has done its very best to help us, and to recognize us and cause others to recognize us.

The Working Group on Minorities has organized three regional seminars for Afrodescendants and they are planning a fourth in Brazil. We want you to know that through these seminars Afrodescendants are coming together as a human family and asking for recognition and human rights protection. We call upon Member States to contribute to the UN Annual Appeal Minorities Project in order to help fund these seminars.

The UN is the greatest law-giver in civilized society. If we cannot call upon the UN, made up of civilized men and women, to grant us protected collective human rights, then who else, can we call upon?

2) Written Statement to the Sub-Commission on the Promotion and Protection of Human Rights Fifth Sixth Session, 26 July to 13 August, 2004 Agenda Item 5 ©) Prevention of discrimination and protection of minorities

We, the Afro descendant minorities throughout the Americas Region and Slavery Diaspora, have been attending and intervening at the Sub-Commission on the Promotion and Protection of Human Rights for eight years. We have been praying for our most basic human rights: our language, culture, and religion; and, we have been repeatedly asking for the recognition of our self-chosen name, Afrodescendants. The Working Group on Minorities has recognized us, the Afro descendant minorities, suffering the lingering effects of slavery.

Both the Sub-Commission and the Commission on Human Rights place minorities on their agenda. They invite minority leaders to travel to Geneva and speak on behalf of their people as delegates of NGOs. Human rights scholars are well aware that we Afro descendant minorities are among the poorest of the poor in the countries in which we live. Yet, from their empty pockets the leaders find the money to come to the U.N. and speak on behalf of their people.

The date when minorities are recognized on the agenda of the Sub-Commission and the Commission on Human Rights is not fixed in the time-table of these Conferences. It seems that even though the United Nations has declared the importance of protecting the rights of minorities, leaders of minority NGOs are often placed in a powerless "minority" position when it comes to speaking at these Conferences.

Frequently the Conferences fall behind in their schedule, and re-scheduling of the minorities agenda item is done without consideration of the minorities themselves. Three times the representative of the NGO All For Reparations and Emancipation, AFRE, has been forced to return home to the United States without delivering his statement himself, due to changes in the time-table.

The United Nations is perceived to be the zenith body of law and order of the world. What other body of law can we call upon? We call upon you, the Sub-Commission. The Sub-Commission has a more respected voice than do we, the minority. As ex-slaves, up from civil death and given birth, what more can we ask, or of whom can we ask that the class of persons fitting the description, minority, have a permanent place on the agenda of the Commission on Human Rights, just as the Indigenous people have their place.

In April of 2004, Secretary-General Kofi Annan spoke to the Commission on Human Rights about the Rwanda genocide and the importance of protecting minorities. On the very day that he was speaking about the importance of protecting minorities, the scheduled time when minority leaders would be able to speak to the Commission on Human Rights was pushed forward over a four day holiday weekend.

This act made the commitment of Secretary-General Annan ring hollow, as minority representatives experienced their powerlessness and their unprotected position within the U.N. The Afro descendant leader, Mr. Silis Muhammad, was unable to stay in Geneva for an extra five days; therefore, he could not speak about the utter destruction of the original identity of his people and their prayer for U.N. recognition and assistance.

We respectfully ask the Sub-Commission to fix the agenda item 5(c) Prevention of discrimination and protection of minorities within the time-table, and make a commitment to minorities that their interventions will be heard on the date that the agenda item is scheduled. We have seen this consideration given to the Indigenous Peoples, and we feel that minorities, in particular Afro descendant minorities, are in a comparable position. Fixing the agenda item 5(c) would be an act of recognition and an example to the Commission on Human Rights.

3) Oral Statement to the 60th Session of the Commission on Human Rights
15 March to 23 April, 2004
Agenda Item 14: Specific groups and individuals: (b) Minorities
Speaker: Mr. Silis Muhammad
Alternate: Ms. Ana Leurinda

I have been asked to speak on behalf of the Afro descendant leader, Mr. Silis Muhammad. Mr. Muhammad could not remain in Geneva over the holiday, beyond the scheduled time allotted for Item 14. Here is his statement:

Due in part to the efforts of the Working Group on Minorities, for the first time in the history of our sojourn, we who are descendants of enslaved Africans collectively took on the identity of Afro descendants at La Ceiba, Honduras in March 2002

We are unlike other people of African descent who live today in different parts of the world. They still have their identity; their mother tongue, and their tribal kinships, and they can enjoy the protection and assistance of their national authorities, if they so choose. But we, who were rendered a stateless people by slavery, were deprived of all of these most precious possessions, and are denied and deprived still of these rights; to enjoy our mother tongue, culture and religion. We cannot reclaim our grandparents – we are orphans in the earth to this day. Four hundred years of forced mixed breeding during slavery and its lingering effects have rendered us unprotected by human rights law.

> We remained quiescent for a long period of time, in the names African American, Afro-American, Blacks, Negro, colored and so on. But today we have taken on the identity "Afro descendants" in some nineteen countries in North, Central and South America and throughout the Slavery Diaspora. Therefore, we Afro descendants request the recognition, protection and assistance of the Commission on Human Rights, and the authorities of the UN. Thank you.

> Mr. Chairman, I have just read the AFRE statement, but I am not the person who should have read it. Wednesday, April 7, minority representatives were scheduled to speak to the Commission on Human Rights under item 14 (b). On that day, when the Secretary General spoke about the importance of protecting minorities, consideration of item 14 was pushed forward into the future. Some leaders of minority communities who travelled to the UN have been forced to return home without speaking because the Commission has fallen behind schedule. This has happened to the Afro descendant leader, Mr. Muhammad, three times. Would the Commission consider protecting leaders of minority communities by fixing item 14 as has been done with item 15? Thank you for your consideration.

4) Written Statement to the 60th Session of the Commission on Human Rights
Agenda Item 14: Specific groups and individuals: (b) Minorities
15 March to 23 April, 2004

We, Afrodescendants, seek placement on the agenda of the Commission on Human Rights. We seek to be placed on the agenda as "New Minorities." We emerged as "New Minorities" during globalization – the present process of economic, political and cultural interconnection, which had its origin after the Cold War. Inasmuch as globalization is the phenomenon that produces new identities, we collectively took on the new identity, Afrodescendants, at La Ceiba, Honduras, in March 2002.

The term Minority has taken on additional meanings. Today the term Minority takes into consideration who has the minority of wealth and power. Thus, today the term Minority has a qualitative value as well as a quantitative value. An analysis in this regard reveals that in all of the Americas and throughout the slavery Diaspora, Afrodescendants are in the minority.

The Working Group on Minorities has placed Afrodescendants in their reports and on their agenda as Afro descendant Minorities. We submit this as a working definition of Afrodescendants: peoples who 1) were forcibly dispossessed of their homeland, Africa; 2) were transported to the Americas and Diaspora for the purpose of enslavement; 3) and were subjected to slavery; 4) were subjected to forced mixed breeding and rape; 5) have experienced, through force, the loss of mother tongue, culture and religion; 6) and have experienced racial discrimination due to lost ties or partially lost ties to their original identity.

For the first time in the history of our sojourn, we collectively have given name to ourselves: Afrodescendants. As Minorities we remained quiescent for a long period of time, in the names African American, Afro-American, Blacks, Negro, Colored, and so on. But today, we collectively have rebuilt our identity in some nineteen countries in North, Central and South America and throughout the slavery Diaspora. Therefore, Afrodescendants are the "New Minorities", and we request to be placed on the agenda of the Commission on Human Rights as such.

5) First Oral Statement to the 10th Session Working Group on Minorities, March 2004
Speaker: Mr. Silis Muhammad
Agenda Item 3 a Afrodescendants

Greetings Mr. Chairman, Members of the Working Group on Minorities. It is a pleasure to be here for the tenth session of the Working Group on Minorities. We have benefitted from your efforts of the past ten years, and we thank you for your dedication.

We, Afrodescendants, emerged as "New Minorities" during globalization – the present process of economic, political and cultural interconnection, which had its origin after the Cold War. Inasmuch as globalization is the phenomenon that produces new identities, we collectively took on the new identity, Afrodescendants, at La Ceiba, Honduras, in March 2002.

In our view, the term Minority has taken on additional meanings. The term has taken into consideration who has the minority of wealth and power. Thus, today the term Minority has a qualitative value as well as a quantitative value. An analysis in this regard reveals that in all of the Americas and throughout the Slavery Diaspora, Afrodescendants are in the minority.

Due in part to the efforts of this Working Group, for the first time in the history of our sojourn, we collectively have given name to ourselves: Afrodescendants. As Minorities we remained quiescent for a long period of time, in the names African American, Afro-American, Blacks, Negro, Colored, and so on. But today, we collectively have rebuilt our identity in some nineteen countries in North, Central and South America and throughout the Slavery Diaspora.

Therefore, Afrodescendants are the "New Minorities." We request that the Working Group on Minorities continue to present us to the Sub-Commission on the Promotion and Protection of Human Rights, and to the United Nations, as such, as we recommend an international decade for the recognition of Minorities.

Thank you.

Second Oral Statement to the 10th Session Working Group on Minorities, March 2004
Speaker: Ms. Cheryl Kyle Sharrief
Agenda Item 3 a   Afrodescendants

Mr. Chairman, distinguished members of this Working Group, participants and observers, I am privileged to be appearing before this distinguished and dedicated body and I thank you for the opportunity to speak in support of the practical realization of the Declaration on the Rights of Minorities.

My name is Cheryl Kyle Sharrief, and I am appearing as a member of All For Reparations and Emancipation and the California Black Chamber of Commerce. For the past 19 years, my profession has been to memorialize and create certified records in judicial, municipal and public sectors. I have been privileged to memorialize the experiences of Afrodescendants as it relates to the lingering effects of slavery and the various political and socioeconomic attempts at overcoming the complete destruction of our identity and the resulting discrimination and marginalization.

We are a new minority, newly awakened to our existence as part of the larger family of Afro descendant Minorities living in the Region of the Americas.

We are awakening to the concept of our right to our original language, culture and religion. We are only intuitively conscious of what has been irreparably stripped from our lost generations which still adversely impacts our present and future generations, and we need a recognized place to fit in order to begin to understand and restore ourselves.

Numerous non-profits are in the process of attempting to establish a cohesive agenda under which to address what amounts to the ethnogenesis of Afrodescendants as a new minority. It is essential that this process continue. The continued efforts of the Working Group on Minorities on our behalf are absolutely essential to us as our process of recovery has only begun. The climb to self awareness is filled with a pain that is stark and unrelenting in its revelation. Recognition is the key to restoring a group that has maintained an evolving identity for centuries. The artistic expressions of Afrodescendants in the U.S. have an influence on many cultures. We Afrodescendants in the U.S. are now in a process of organizing ourselves toward collective decision-making. The efforts of the Working Group on Minorities are essential in assisting us in our process.

We thank you for your working papers and for your Regional Seminars. We in the United States know of your efforts through the internet and through our own national conferences. The Working Group on Minorities has made itself a part of our history, and we urge governments to support this Working Group in order that its great work might continue.

Maintaining the mechanism that enables people to directly and personally intervene with the Working Group is paramount in its task of promoting and having practical realization of the Declaration on the Rights of Minorities.

Third Oral Statement to the 10th Session Working Group on Minorities, March 2004
Speaker: Ms. Raushana Karriem
Agenda Item 3 a   Afrodescendants
Organization - National Commission For Reparations

Mr. Chairman, distinguished members of the Working Group, NGO's and observers, I am privileged to be appearing before this distinguished panel of experts, to speak in concert for the support of the practical realization of the Declaration on the Rights of Minorities.

> I am Raushana Karriem, Senior Commissioner of the National Commission for Reparations, Atlanta, Georgia U.S.A. For the past 32 years, I have been active in seeking justice for Afrodescendants.

The legacies of plantation slavery still haunt Afrodescendants in the Americas. When released from chattel slavery, Afrodescendants in North America were released penniless, naked, ignorant, hungry and landless, unlike their counterparts in Jamaica, Haiti, etc. Today after over 100 years of menial emancipation, Afrodescendants are often seen in the same pitiable condition.

During slavery our human rights were systematically destroyed. After our kidnap and capture, we were separated from our various tribes and put with others, so as to insure we would not to be able to communicate with each other. The mother tongue of the Afrodescendant was lost forever, which is essential to one's identity.

After reaching the shores of the Americas, husbands, wives, children, mothers and fathers were sold to different owners and bred like animals to produce strong workers, who were again sold to the highest bidder at the whim or convenience of their masters.. This was deliberately done, and resulted in the destruction of black ancestral culture and religion, which the Afrodescendant will never regain. Thus, Afrodescendants have the distinction of being the only people on earth who can never hope to find their specific ancestral roots, language, culture or religion. It is lost to us forever.

The UN Universal Declaration of Human Rights, states that every human being on earth is entitled to these human rights. The Working Group on Minorities should be commended for their attention and input into these centuries old and present day injustices that still plague Afrodescendants. The cry for justice by Afro descendants has now been reverberated around the world, and is being heard by the people of the world. The Working Group on Minorities have provided this forum.

Written and Oral Statements to the UN in 2003

Statements delivered in 2003 were heard and responded to by the UN.

Written and Oral Statements to the United Nations in 2003

Table of Contents

1. Oral Statement to the 55th Session of the Sub-Commission on the Promotion and Protection of Human Rights

2. Written Statement to the 55th Session of the Sub-Commission on the Promotion and Protection of Human Rights

3. Oral Statements to the 9th Session of the Working Group on Minorities (three statements)

4. Oral Statement to the 59th Session of the Commission on Human Rights

5. Written Statements to the 59th Session of the Commission on Human Rights (two statements)

1. Oral Statement to the Sub-Commission on the Promotion and Protection of Human Rights Fifty Fifth Session, 28 July to 15 August, 2003 Agenda item 5 (c) Prevention of discrimination and protection of minorities.
Speaker: Mr. Silis Muhammad (alternate: Ms. Ana Leurinda)

We, the Afrodescendant Minorities throughout the Slavery Diaspora, have experienced total destruction of our collective human rights: original identity - language, culture and religion, as articulated in the Declaration on the Rights of Minorities and in Article 27 of the ICCPR. We once were families of African Nations, but today our blood is mixed with the blood of the slave masters. We speak his mother tongue instead of our own.

We are today the living example of the lingering effects of slavery, scattered across the Americas and the Slavery Diaspora. The sweet smell of freedom to choose our destiny is still snatched from our Life. The rights of Afrodescendant peoples are not legally recognized by the UN General Assembly; thereby, we do not have the respect nor the protection of the UN as do other human families.

We began, in 1997, bringing our prayers to the Sub-Commission, and we know today that it is through the resolutions of the Sub-Commission and the diligent efforts of the Working Group on Minorities that we, Afrodescendant Minorities, approach restoration of our collective human rights.

The 9th Session of the Working Group on Minorities has decided to place Afrodescendant Minorities on its agenda for 2004, acknowledging that we are minorities in the States in which we exist, either as numerical minorities or minorities with regard to possession of wealth and power.

We are recognized thereby as new minorities. We seek official recognition that we are new minorities, from the Sub-Commission and all bodies of the UN.

We support the recommendations of the 9th Session of the Working Group on Minorities for a second regional seminar for Afrodescendants in the Americas Region as a follow-up to the highly successful La Ceiba Seminar of 2001.

We urge the Sub-Commission to place its full support behind the Working Group on Minorities, and establish an International Year for Minorities with a Decade for Minorities to follow, as recommended by the Working Group on Minorities.

Thank you.

2. Written Statement to the Sub-Commission on the Promotion and Protection of Human Rights Fifty Fifth Session, 28 July to 15 August, 2003 Agenda Item 5 (c), Prevention of discrimination and protection of minorities

Afrodescendants are peoples who have their roots in Africa, who have been forcibly transported to the Americas for slavery and have experienced the loss of their original identity, language, culture and religion, as articulated in the Declaration on the Rights of Minorities and in Article 27 of the International Covenant on Civil and Political Rights.

In the countries in which Afrodescendants reside, we are in the position of minorities: either minorities numerically or minorities with regard to possession of money and power. In 1997 the Sub-Commission on the Promotion and Protection of Human Rights placed Afrodescendant issues before the Working Group on Minorities, and since 1998 the Working Group on Minorities has given great expertise, time and consideration to our issues.

Through the efforts of the Working Group on Minorities we Afrodescendants have begun to establish a foundation upon which we can proceed in our efforts, as recognition, restoration and reconciliation are our primary concerns. We urge the Sub-Commission to strongly support the efforts of the Working Group on Minorities on our behalf.

We fully support the decisions of the 9th Session of the Working Group on Minorities with regard to Afrodescendant minorities, and we are very grateful to the experts of this Working Group, for they are listening and responding to us, the descendants who continue to suffer the effects of slavery.

3. First Oral Statement to the 9th Session of the Working Group on Minorities, May 2003
Speaker: Mr. Silis Muhammad

Greetings Mr. Chairman. The Afrodescendant people, throughout the Slavery Diaspora, are, to this date, struggling for the protection of the UN. We are a diverse people, we know, in the lingering effects of slavery, and speaking no one common language. Albeit, we know, we are one common people seeking recognition of our inherent human rights.

We, Afrodescendants, have experienced total destruction of our essence: our original identity, language, culture and religion, as articulated in the Declaration on the Rights of Minorities and in Article 27 of the ICCPR.

These rights are denied us by systematically eliminating from our minds our mother tongue, culture and religion. By denying us these rights, generation after generation, in our homes and in our schools, the U.S. Government, in particular, destroys us mentally, and this is in breach of both the Minorities Declaration and Article 27.

These rights are an impossibility to recapture. The damages to us cannot be repaired due to forced mixed breeding during 400 years of slavery. The injury lingers on amidst us, collectively, to this day. We have been cross-bred by the slave masters, with no more regard than the regard given to animals. In America the slave masters cross-bred horses and donkeys in order to get a mule, which they used for plowing. We, like that mule, are a mixture of different people speaking different languages. We do not know what language we should speak, and tracing DNA cannot correct our dilemma.

We live either as numerical minorities, or minorities with regard to wealth and power, throughout the Region of the Americas and the Slavery Diaspora. We are the powerless and wealth-less minority, especially in the Islands, South, Central and North America and in the Slavery Diaspora. We are therefore new minorities, and we ask the UN to officially recognize us.

The children of the slave masters are reaping immense benefits from slavery, sanctioned by their Governments. By placing Afrodescendants on the UN agenda as recognized minorities, the UN and its Member States will give justice to us, and justify us as being human beings, equal to the slave master's children.

The ex-slaves are rising from a state of civil death. Other people of African descent, whose ancestors were not subject to slavery, still have their original identity, mother tongue and culture. It is axiomatic. We do not. The Working Group on People of African Descent has, in its first two sessions, failed to recognize this fact: that we have experienced civil death, and that we are now experiencing ethnogenesis.

I recommend that the Working Group on Minorities organize a second Regional Seminar for Afrodescendant Minorities in the Americas Region, similar to the very beneficial seminar, that was attended by our leaders from 19 countries, in La Ceiba, Honduras. Afrodescendant leaders wish to continue the work begun at that Seminar.

In closing, we, Afrodescendants, believe that United Nations protection of our collective human rights will place us on a path of recompense. We would like to thank the Working Group on Minorities for consistently demonstrating its concern for Afrodescendant Minorities.

Second Oral Statement to 9th Session of the Working Group on Minorities
Speaker: Silis Muhammad
Agenda Item 5: Other Matters

Mr. Chairman, members of the Working Group on Minorities. I would like to thank you for your decision to hold a follow-up seminar to the La Ceiba Seminar for Afrodescendants. We will support this decision fully, in any way we can, and we recommend that, if possible, the second seminar be held in Brazil. I would also like to thank the Working Group for their willingness to prepare working papers for the next session. We thank you for responding to the needs of the Minorities and their recommendations.

Third Oral Statement to the 9th Session of the Working Group on Minorities
Speaker: Harriett AbuBakr Muhammad

Greetings Mr. Chairman, members of the Working Group on Minorities. I am grateful to be here again this year in order to learn more about how we Afrodescendants might utilize the Declaration on the Rights of Minorities to bring about justice for ourselves and an end to injustice in the future.

My name is Harriett AbuBakr Muhammad. I represent the National Commission for Reparations. Because I am an attorney at law, I have looked to international human rights law for justice for my people. Since our first UN communication in 1994, we, the descendants of enslaved Africans in the Americas, have been pressing a claim that international human rights law has been violated. We have been denied and deprived of our original identity, mother tongue, culture and religion. For us, the slavery experience is not in the past, as the lingering effects of slavery are within us - permanently. And in addition to this permanent damage, deliberate acts to keep us from rising, collectively, have continued, and are continuing into the present time in violation of international law.

We began to try to establish ourselves collectively around the 1930's. Our movement became very strong in the 1960's. During the 60's and 70's, unknown to many people outside North America, there was a human rights movement running counter to the much publicized civil rights movement. I have deep personal experience of our human rights movement and the destabilization and destruction of our movement by the U.S. Government's infamous Counter Intelligence Program. During that time I was a member of the family of the Honorable Elijah Muhammad. This great leader taught us, even then, that what we need is human rights. Some of you may have become familiar with his human rights efforts through his spokesman, Malcolm X.

Due to the deliberate acts of the U.S. Government from the 1950's to the present, which we claim are in violation of Article 27 of the ICCPR, we are still today forced to engage in a struggle to establish ourselves internationally, with a UN recognized identity. The world has not yet clearly acknowledged that we exist.

Recently we have had to face another area of struggle within the UN. There seems to be a persistent desire to group us within the same category as other people of African descent who have not experienced the destruction of their original identity, mother tongue, culture and religion. We deeply appreciate our roots in Africa, but this appreciation should not prevent us from telling the world that we have, through force, lost our original identity. As this Working Group knows, people of African descent who have not experienced slavery are able to tell you where they come from, what their heritage is, what their original language is, what God their ancestors believed in. We cannot know these things - ever. What a terrible loss for us - and the world seems to want to gloss it over.

Our task has been to come together with each other, recognize ourselves and re-claim an identity that befits us. On our own, and with the help of the Working Group on Minorities, we have done this. Now we want the UN to clearly acknowledge that the Afrodescendant Minorities are a specific human family, emerging as a result of slavery, destruction of identity and forced mixed breeding. The UN can recognize our existence in the language of its documents and by placing our issues on appropriate agendas for discussion.

Even though the UN is to be applauded for its efforts against racism, and the establishment of a moral argument for reparations in the documents of the World Conference Against Racism, some of the outcomes of this Conference, including the Working Group on People of African Descent, have not yet heard our prayers for official UN recognition of our existence. We know that our rise, our ethnogenesis, is not easily understood, and we thank the Working Group on Minorities for their exceptional loyalty to human rights, and their immediate understanding and response to our first intervention some six years ago. We have come from death to life, and we are grateful to those who have seen and acknowledged this truth.

In conclusion, we agree with Mr. Silis Muhammad that a second Regional Seminar for Afrodescendant Minorities in the Americas Region would be beneficial to us. We ask the Working Group on Minorities to continue to validate our self-chosen identity in its documents, and use any other means available to it, to place the fact of our existence before the UN and the world. We are the Afrodescendant Minorities.

4. Oral Statement to the 59th Session of the Commission on Human Rights
17 March to 25 April, 2003
Agenda Item 15
Speaker: Mr. Silis Muhammad

Greetings Mr. Chairman. The Afrodescendant people, throughout the Slavery Diaspora, are, to this date, struggling for UN recognition of our inherent human rights. We Afrodescendants have experienced total destruction of our essence: our original identity, language and religion. The U.S. Secretary of State is a classic example of how weapons of mass destruction are being used against us. We now know, weapons of mass destruction can destroy the person physically, or destroy the person mentally. He, to this day, is denied by the country he serves, the use of his own language, culture and religion. These rights, as articulated in Article 27 of the ICCPR, are denied us generation after generation, and this denial is tantamount to weapons of mass destruction of the mind.

Other people of African descent whose ancestors were not subject to slavery, still have their original identity. We do not.

We believe that UN recognition of our inherent human rights will place us on a path of recompense: if ever we are to be equal to our slave masters' children. We ask you to place our issue on the agenda of the Sub-Commission and in the hands of the Working Group on Minorities.

5. (First) Written Statement to the 59th Session of the Commission on Human Rights
17 March to 25 April, 2003
Agenda Item 14: Specific groups and individuals: (b) Minorities

Four hundred years of the trans-Atlantic slave trade, plantation slavery, and the lingering effects of slavery have caused us, the Afrodescendants, to be left out of the UN system. Other people of African descent living in the Diaspora whose ancestors were not subjected to slavery in the Americas Region, still have their original identity and their bond with others of their family, tribe or nation. We do not. Thus we do not have collective human rights (original language, culture and religion), as articulated in Article 27 of the ICCPR.

Our collective human rights were utterly destroyed due to forced denial of our original identity and forced mixed breeding during slavery. Today we are no longer bonded together by the mother tongue, culture and religion of our ancestors. We, the Afrodescendant minorities in the Americas Region and slavery Diaspora, wish to reconstitute ourselves and reconstruct our lost ties with UN assistance. We seek to be recognized by the UN as one people, and we seek to have our collective human rights restored as the first step in granting us reparations for slavery and its lingering effects.

Afrodescendants is a name that we have chosen for ourselves. We chose this name during the process leading up to the World Conference Against Racism, and chose it again when Afrodescendant leaders from 19 countries met in La Ceiba, Honduras at a seminar organized by the UN Working Group on Minorities, which is a working group of the Sub-Commission on the Promotion and Protection of Human Rights.

In La Ceiba we began to define Afrodescendants as peoples who have their roots in Africa, who have been forcibly transported to the Americas for slavery, and have experienced the loss of their original identity, language and religion, and as a result suffer discrimination.

The experts of the Working Group on Minorities are aware that we Afrodescendants are experiencing, in reality, the process of ethnogenesis: a word that describes the coming to life again of a people who have been scattered, forcibly cut off, severed; now seemingly assimilated, within the countries of their domicile. This Working Group has been studying and assisting Afrodescendant minorities for six years under the direction of the Sub-Commission. Through the efforts of the Working Group on Minorities we have begun to establish a foundation upon which we Afrodescendants can proceed in our efforts, as recognition, restoration and reconciliation are our primary concerns.

We sincerely appreciate the decisions made by the Commission on Human Rights on our behalf, and we respectfully ask the Commission to consider our recommendation: we recommend that the Commission on Human Rights pass a resolution asking the Sub-Commission to place Afrodescendants on their agenda. We feel that restoration of the human rights of Afrodescendants is best placed in the capable hands of the Sub-Commission on the Promotion and Protection of Human Rights and the Working Group on Minorities.

(Second) Written Statement to the 59th Session of the Commission on Human Rights 17 March to 25 April, 2003 Agenda Item 6: Racism, Racial Discrimination, Xenophobia and all Forms of Discrimination

The 58th Session of the Commission on Human Rights in its resolution 2002/68 decided to establish a Working Group on People of African Descent. This Working Group of five experts has conducted two sessions. In its 59th Session the

Commission on Human Rights will hear and consider recommendations of this Working Group.

Since 1994 the leader of All For Reparations and Emancipation (AFRE), Mr. Silis Muhammad, has been intervening at the United Nations on behalf of the Afrodescendants in the Americas Region and the slavery Diaspora. Because of his continuing concern with the human rights of Afrodescendants, AFRE has taken a strong interest in the newly formed Working Group on People of African Descent.

In November of 2002 AFRE invited a group of Afrodescendant leaders to attend and participate in the first session of the Working Group on People of African Descent. Then, after much careful deliberation, we decided not to attend the second session. With the greatest respect and appreciation for the decisions of the Commission on Human Rights undertaken on behalf of Afrodescendants, we ask that the Commission consider our position, stated as follows:

AFRE is concerned with restoration of our human rights, their recognition and reparations for Afrodescendants. We Afrodescendants are a people who have our roots in Africa, who have been forcibly transported to the Americas for slavery and who have experienced total destruction of our essence: our original identity, language, and religion, and as a result we suffer discrimination.

Although we appreciate the efforts of the Working Group on People of African Descent, we understand that this Working Group has received its mandate from the Commission on Human Rights. We refer in particular to CHR Resolution 2002/68 (d) which asks the Working Group to elaborate a proposal for a mechanism to monitor and promote all of the human rights of people of African descent. We

Afrodescendants do not possess human rights, as articulated in Article 27 of the ICCPR, for the Working Group to monitor or promote. Other people of African descent living in the Diaspora whose ancestors were not subjected to slavery in the Americas Region still have their original identity and their bond with others of their family, tribe or nation. We do not. Thus our human rights cannot be monitored or promoted. They must first be restored.

Afrodescendants are, to this date, no longer bonded together by the mother tongue, culture and religion of our ancestors due to forced denial of our original identity and forced mixed breeding during slavery. Our collective human rights (original language, culture and religion), as articulated in Article 27 of the ICCPR, were utterly destroyed.

In the countries in which Afrodescendants reside, we are in the position of minorities: either minorities numerically or minorities with regard to possession of money and power. In 1997 the Sub-Commission on the Promotion and Protection of Human Rights placed Afrodescendant issues before the Working Group on Minorities, and since 1998 the Working Group on Minorities has given great expertise, time and consideration to Afrodescendant issues. They have organized three regional seminars and they have brought in a number of scholars on issues such as autonomous and semi-autonomous arrangements.

We believe that the lack of collective human rights, the lack of UN recognition, and reparations must be addressed in order for the very grave injuries suffered to date by Afrodescendants to be resolved at their root.

We do not intend to mortgage the future of the generations of Afrodescendants to come. The leader of AFRE and other Afrodescendant leaders from the U.S. who support our position, feel that reparations must begin with restoration and UN recognition of our collective human rights. We do not agree to reparations only in the form of development money, affirmative action, examination of the records of slavery history, setting up monuments to honor our experience and so on. While these things may be helpful in improving the condition of our people, we Afrodescendants will still be a people without human rights recognition under UN law.

We Afrodescendants seek to be recognized by the UN as one people, however diverse, under our self-chosen name, living as minorities (either numerical or economic/power minorities) throughout the Region of the Americas and the slavery Diaspora. Because our issue is restoration of collective human rights, we believe it is best placed in the hands of the experts of the Sub-Commission on the Promotion and Protection of Human Rights and the Working Group on Minorities.

Written and Oral Statements to the UN in 2002

Statements delivered in 2002 were heard and responded to by the UN.

Documents of 2002 in order of presentation:

1. Oral Statement to the 54th Session of the Sub-Commission on the Promotion and Protection of Human Rights

2. Written Statement to the 54th Session of the Sub-Commission on the Promotion and Protection of Human Rights 2002

3. Oral Statement to the 8th Session of the Working Group on Minorities (English)

4. Oral Statement to the 8th Session of the Working Group on Minorities (Spanish)

5. Written Statement to the 58th Session of the Commission on Human Rights 2002

6. Oral Statement to the 58th Session of the Commission on Human Rights

1) Oral Statement to the Sub-Commission on the Promotion and Protection of Human Rights

Fifty-Fourth Session (2002)

Agenda Item 5 (c)

In 1997 and 1998 the Sub-Commission passed two resolutions of concern to us. The first called upon the Working Group on Minorities to consider how the Sub-Commission in its future work might usefully address the continuing legal, political and economic legacies of the African slave trade, as experienced by Black communities throughout the Americas. The second urged the Working Group on Minorities to include on its agenda an item on issues related to the legacies of the slave trade on the Black communities throughout the Americas.

At the 4th Session of the Working Group on Minorities we saw that the protections offered minorities under Article 27 of the ICCPR did not apply to us, the descendants of enslaved Africans, for we have been denied a collective international identity and denied our original mother tongues, cultures and religions, which is the total destruction of our essence, although some of us are unaware.

One of the decisions of the Working Group on Minorities was to assign Mr. Jose Bengoa to write a paper on the existence and recognition of minorities. This paper was a tremendous benefit to us, for it started the process of our recognition as minorities undergoing ethnogenesis.

In 2001 the Working Group participated in a Saturday session held in Geneva, and in a Conference held in Montreal, Canada in order to listen to our issues. The

Working Group also listened to our issues at the World Conference Against Racism in Durban and at a historic meeting in La Ceiba, Honduras.

In Honduras it was shown that "minorities" is an evolving term: it could denote who has the minority of power and wealth, and clearly the Afro Descendants are usually the minority in that respect. Also in Honduras we Afro Descendants, of some 19 countries, recognized ourselves and decided, by concensus, that we wish to be recognized by the UN as Afro Descendant Minorities.

The Working Group on Minorities has acknowledged our decision to be recognized as Afro Descendant Minorities. We ask the Sub-Commission to acknowledge our decision also.

In conclusion, we recognize that as minorities we do not have full equality before the law due to the total destruction of our essence, our identity, which, as we have seen, is the loss of our identity internationally. We believe the reinstatement of us to the human family, and reparation can take place with the continued effort of the Sub-Commission and the Working Group on Minorities.

Mr. Silis Muhammad

2) Written Statement to the Sub-Commission on the Promotion and Protection of Human Rights

Fifty-Fourth Session

Provisional Agenda Item 5: Prevention of Discrimination

(c) Prevention of Discrimination and Protection of Minorities

August 2002

The following statement is offered by Mr. Silis Muhammad on behalf of the Afro Descendant Minority in the United States of America.

We know that it is through the resolutions of the Sub-Commission and the diligent efforts of the Working Group on Minorities that we Afro Descendants approach collective human rights. We wish to continue to trust the Sub-Commission and the expertise of the Working Group on Minorities.

In 1997 the Sub-Commission on the Promotion and Protection of Human Rights passed resolution, #E/CN.4/SUB.2/RES/1997/5, in which the Sub-Commission called upon the Working Group on Minorities to consider how the Sub-Commission in its future work might usefully address the continuing legal, political and economic legacies of the African slave trade, as experienced by Black communities throughout the Americas. Following that resolution, in 1998, the Working Group on Minorities invited us to attend their 4th Session. We did attend that Session, and we have continued to attend and offer statements to all sessions of the Sub-Commission, the Commission on Human Rights and the Working Group on Minorities since that time.

At the 4th Session of the Working Group on Minorities we examined the Declaration on the Rights of Minorities, and it appeared to us that the so-called African Americans did not fit in the United Nations system. We had been told we are "minorities" by the United States Government, but we saw that we did not enjoy such recognition internationally. We saw that the protections offered minorities under Article 27 of the International Covenant on Civil and Political Rights and under the UN Declaration on the Rights of Minorities did not apply to us, for we do not have our original identity, our mother tongue, culture or religion. At that first meeting one of the esteemed members of the Working Group on Minorities said, "We will have to find out where you fit." Today I thank him. Over the years this Working Group has demonstrated that it is not willing to leave us out.

One of the decisions of the 4th Session of the Working Group on Minorities was to assign a member of the Working Group to write a paper on the existence and recognition of minorities. The paper was presented in the year 2000 as document #E/CN.4/Sub.2/AC.5/2000/WP.2. This expert paper has been of tremendous benefit to us, for it started the process of our recognition as minorities undergoing ethnogenesis. During the 52nd Session of the Sub-Commission we expected to hear a presentation of the paper, and we were disappointed when it was not presented. We continue to ask the experts of the Sub-Commission to discuss our issues on the Sub-Commission floor and consider this Working Paper of the Working Group on Minorities, which we believe offers the most advanced understanding of our situation.

In 1998 the Sub-Commission passed resolution, #E/CN.4/SUB.2/RES/1998/24, in which the Sub-Commission urged the Working Group on Minorities to include on its agenda an item on issues related to the legacies of the slave trade on the Black communities throughout the Americas. In response to this Sub-Commission resolution, the 5th Session of the Working Group on Minorities placed African descendants in the Americas on its agenda. This was the first time, to my knowledge, that we were placed on the agenda of any UN meeting.

From that time forward the Working Group on Minorities has continued to address our issues in a most forthright manner. In the year 2000 the Working Group announced that it would hold regional seminars to study the issues of African descendants in the Americas. In 2001 the Working Group participated in a special Saturday session held in Geneva, and in a Conference held in Montreal, Canada in order to listen specifically to our issues. The Working Group also listened to our issues at the World Conference Against Racism in Durban.

Then, in 2002 the Working Group on Minorities held a long awaited and historic meeting in La Ceiba, Honduras. At that meeting we recognized and affirmed that "minority" is an evolving term that can be used creatively. Rather than looking at majority or minority with respect to numbers only, we looked at the terms with respect to who has the majority of the power and wealth, and who has the minority of the power and wealth, and South Africa is a great example of this axiom. When minority is seen in that light then we, all of us who are descendants of enslaved Africans, are in the minority.

In Honduras we descendants, as a newly emerging family of some 240 million souls, were able to determine the name by which we would like to be known in the UN. We are now in agreement that we recognize ourselves and we wish to be recognized by the UN as Afro Descendants. A definition of the term Afro Descendants is forthcoming from us. At the Honduras meeting we also made the decision, by consensus, to approach the UN under the category of Minorities.

The Working Group on Minorities has acknowledged our decision to be recognized as Afro Descendant Minorities. We ask the Sub-Commission to acknowledge our decision also. We urge the Sub-Commission to strongly support the efforts of the Working Group on Minorities on our behalf, as we see this Working Group as having gained invaluable expertise on our issues. Through the efforts of the Working Group we have begun to establish a foundation upon which we can proceed in our efforts, as recognition, restoration and reconciliation are our primary concerns.

In conclusion, we recognize that as Minorities we do not have full equality before the law due to the intentional destruction of our original identity, and yet we believe appropriate reparation and restoration can take place with the continued effort of the Sub-Commission and the Working Group on Minorities.

3) Oral Statement to the Working Group on Minorities

8th Session, May 2002

Greetings Mr. Chairman and Members of the Working Group on Minorities. We know that it is through the diligent efforts of the Working Group on Minorities that we Afro Descendants approach collective human rights, and we wish to continue to trust the expertise of this Working Group.

If we learned anything in La Ceiba, Honduras we learned that minority is an evolving term that can be used creatively. Rather than looking at majority or minority with respect to numbers only, we looked at the terms with respect to who has the majority of the power and wealth, and who has the minority of the power and wealth. When minority is seen in that light then we, all of us Afro Descendants, are in the minority, and South Africa is a great example of this axiom.

It has been five years since I first came before this group. At that time I had examined the Declaration on the Rights of Minorities, and it appeared to me that African Americans did not fit in the UN system. I felt that the protections offered minorities did not apply to us, for we do not have our original identity, our mother tongue, culture or religion. At that first meeting one of the esteemed members of this group said, "We will have to find out where you fit." Today I thank him. Over the years this Working Group has demonstrated that it is not willing to leave us out.

In 1998 the Working Group on Minorities assigned one of its members to write a paper on the existence and recognition of minorities. The paper has been of tremendous benefit, for it started the process of our recognition as minorities undergoing ethnogenesis. Today I thank the esteemed expert who wrote that paper.

In 1999 the Working Group on Minorities placed African descendants in the Americas on its agenda. This was the first time, to my knowledge, that we were placed on the agenda of any UN meeting. In the year 2000 the Working Group announced that it would hold regional seminars to study the issues of African Americans. In 2001 the Working Group participated in a special Saturday session in order to listen to our issues. In 2002 the Working Group on Minorities held a historic meeting in Honduras where we, as a newly emerging family of some 240 million souls, were able to determine the name by which we would like to be known in the UN. We are now in agreement that we will approach the UN as Afro Descendant Minorities.

Mr. Silis Muhammad

4) Intervención presentada en el Grupo de Trabajo sobre Minorías

8ª sesión, Mayo 2002

Les presento Sr. Presidente y Miembros del Grupo de Trabajo sobre Minorías mis cordiales saludos. Sabemos que gracias a los diligentes esfuerzos de este Grupo, que todos nosotros Afro-
descendientes, colaboramos estrechamente por los derechos humanos colectivos, y esperamos seguir confiando con
la experiencia de este Grupo de Trabajo.

Sí algo aprendimos en
La Ceiba, Honduras, es que las minorías forman un conjunto de creatividad.
En vez de mirar solamente al número con respecto a
la mayoría o a
la minoría, miramos al conjunto con respecto a quien tiene la mayoría del poder y de
la riqueza y quien tiene la minoría del poder y
la riqueza. Cuando la minoría es vista
con transparencia, entonces, todos nosotros afro descendientes pertenecemos a
la minoría y África del Sur es un gran ejemplo.

Han transcurrido 5 años desde mi primera venida a este Grupo. Desde entonces yo revisé la Declaración de los Derechos de las Minorías y me pareció que los Afro-americanos no

95

se encontraban dentro del Sistema de las Naciones Unidas. Sentí que la protección dada
a las Minorías no encajaba con nosotros, al
no tener nuestra propia identidad, nuestra lengua materna, nuestra cultura, religión. En esa primera reunión, uno de los estimados miembros de este Grupo dijo "tendremos que buscar una salida para que puedan entrar". Ahora, se
lo agradezco. A través de los años este Grupo de Trabajo nos ha demostrado que no nos quiere dejar afuera.

En 1998,
el Grupo de Trabajo sobre Minorías asignó a uno de sus miembros a escribir un informe sobre la existencia y
el reconocimiento de las minorías. Este informe ha sido de gran beneficio,
y así comenzó el proceso de nuestro reconocimiento como minorías. Hoy, le doy las gracias
al estimado experto que escribió dicho informe.

En 1999,
EL Grupo de Trabajo sobre Minorías tenía en su agenda
a los Afro-descendientes de América. Esta fue la primera vez, a mi conocer que se puso en la Agenda
de las reuniones del Sistema de Naciones Unidas. En
el año 2000,
el Grupo de Trabajo anunció que se formarían Grupos de Trabajo Regionales para estudiar los temas de los Afro-descendientes. En el 2001,
el Grupo de Trabajo participó, durante un sábado en una reunión muy especial para discutir los temas de afro-descendientes. En el 2002,
el Grupo de Trabajo sobre Minorías celebró una reunión histórica en Honduras,
y dio como resultado una nueva familia emergente de
240 millones de almas, que acordaron determinar el nombre p

or el cual les gustaría ser llamados dentro del marco de las Naciones Unidas, en el Grupo de Trabajo sobre Minorías como Afro-descendientes.

5) Written Statement to the 58th Session of the Commission on Human Rights under

Provisional Agenda Item 14. Specific groups and individuals (b) Minorities

March/April 2002

1. The United Nations has not, as yet, recognized us: we who are the African American peoples or nations in North, Central and South America and the Diaspora. Four hundred years of plantation slavery and its lingering effects have left us deprived of and denied our mother tongue and thus outside a definite place within the UN system. For the past six years, on behalf of the African American people in the United States, Mr. Silis Muhammad has traveled to the UN at Geneva to deliver numerous prayers for recognition and restoration. He has asked that the UN to find or make a category in which we, the African American, will fit; for at present, we have no collective human rights.

2. In the Americas Region and throughout the Diaspora we, who are the descendants of slaves, are filled with dissatisfaction, and many of us do not know its source. The African American people in the United States are perhaps the first to recognize the source of our pain and the gravity of our situation. We know that we have been forcibly cut off, severed from our original identity: our mother tongue, religion and culture: those very things that give life to

peoples. We have been as "dead" for 400 years. Today we are experiencing, in reality, the process of ethnogenesis: a word that describes the coming to life again of a people who have been scattered, forcibly cut off, severed; now seemingly assimilated, within the country of our domicile.

3. We have cried out in many ways over many years for the restoration of our dignity as a people. Yet the U.S. Government and other nations commit, daily, the international wrongful act of denying our existence while claiming respect for human rights. It is our desire to reconstitute ourselves and reconstruct our lost ties, with UN assistance. It is also our desire to receive reparations from the U.S. Government for the ongoing loss of our mother tongue and our internationally recognized political identity.

4. We recognize that the United Nations has made some attempts to assist us. In 1997 the Sub-Commission on the Promotion and Protection of Human Rights passed a resolution, #E/CN.4/SUB.2/RES/1997/5, in which the Sub-Commission called upon the Working Group on Minorities to consider how the Sub-Commission in its future work might usefully address the continuing legal, political and economic legacies of the African slave trade, as experienced by Black communities throughout the Americas. In 1998 the Sub-Commission again passed a resolution, #E/CN.4/SUB.2/RES/1998/24, in which the Sub-Commission urged the Working Group on Minorities to include on its agenda an item on issues related to the legacies of the slave trade on the Black communities throughout the Americas.

5. The Working Group on Minorities is aware that we, the African American people, do not fit into a category within the UN system due to the immoral slavery and its illegal lingering effects: especially the deliberate acts of the U.S.

Government. In 1998 the Working Group assigned Mr. Jose Bengoa to write a working paper on the existence and recognition of minorities. In the year 2000 this working paper, #E/CN.4/Sub.2/AC.5/2000/WP.2, was presented to the Working Group on Minorities, and accepted by the group. In the paper Mr. Bengoa demonstrated an astute understanding of the ethnogenesis of African Americans. Regrettably this distinguished paper has not been selected for presentation on the Sub-Commission floor.

6. To date, the Sub-Commission has not invited the Working Group on Minorities to report specifically on the work and study that it has been engaged in regarding African Americans. Consequently, the Sub-Commission has not addressed the continuing legal, political and economic legacies of the African slave trade as it had in 1997 indicated a desire to do. While we appreciate and highly value the efforts of the Working Group on Minorities on our behalf, we believe that little progress can be made in our recognition and restoration without the continued interest of the Sub-Commission.

7. Therefore we urgently recommend that the Commission on Human Rights pass a resolution requesting that the Sub-Commission on the Promotion and Protection of Human Rights place African Americans on its agenda, alongside Indigenous Peoples and Minorities. Placement on the agenda of the Sub-Commission would be a welcome first step in official UN recognition of the African Americans.

8. As the World Conference Against Racism demonstrated to the world, African Americans in the Americas Region and the Diaspora are united in a mass call for reparations. In response to the mass call for reparations, the World Conference, in it's Program of Action, made a request of the Commission on

Human Rights as follows: "7. Requests the Commission on Human Rights to consider establishing a working group or other mechanism of the United Nations to study the problems of racial discrimination faced by people of African descent living in the African Diaspora and make proposals for the elimination of racial discrimination against people of African descent."

9. The World Conference Against Racism, in paragraph 14 of its Declaration, recognizes that for African Americans, racial discrimination is a consequence of slavery. Thus we would welcome a working group or other mechanism of the Commission on Human Rights if the mechanism has as its primary focus the lingering effects of slavery, and the restoration of our people. In particular, we would request that the proposed working group or other mechanism focus upon the establishment of category in which the UN and world community can recognize African Americans collectively and provide for reparations and restoration of the human rights of the African American people. We would also urge the Commission on Human Rights to take advantage of the work that has already been accomplished by the Working Group on Minorities on behalf of African Americans, and in particular the scholarship of Mr. Jose Bengoa.

10. In our view, and in the view of the organizations and leaders that support us, the dissatisfaction of our people will not be addressed with solutions that are ultimately superficial. The United Nations, and the national governments that have authority over us, cannot repair the damage done by slavery with reparations such as development money, affirmative action or anti-discrimination laws alone. We have lost our original identity and we have been forced to assume the identity of our slave masters. One man cannot live in another man's "skin." It is against nature, and inhumane. Our

dissatisfaction will increase until our ethnogenesis is recognized and our human rights are restored.

11. At the World Conference Against Racism the U.S. Government turned its back and walked out on our cries with the same disdain that it has shown internally toward our cries for 400 years. Today we turn to the Commission on Human Rights and the world community with increasing urgency. We fear that if our prayer for UN recognition of our existence is not heard, and if restoration does not take place, we will not be able to hold back a flood of anger that the world only glimpsed in Durban, South Africa.

6) Oral Statement to the 58th Session of the Commission on Human Rights

Agenda Item 14 (b) Specific Groups and Individuals: Minorities

March/April 2002

We, the Afro Descendant Minority living in the United States of America, would like to thank the United Nations for requesting that the Commission on Human Rights consider establishing a working group or other mechanism of the United Nations to study the problems of racial discrimination faced by people of African descent living in the African Diaspora and make proposals for the elimination of racial discrimination against people of African descent.

While we appreciate the encouragement to States to deal with the problems Afro Descendants face, a study of the problems of racial discrimination would not address the root problem, especially the negation of the essence of the victims. Racial discrimination is just the end product of our having suffered through slavery. Therefore, it is not enough to address the issue of discrimination ONLY. Justice calls for an examination of the entire cause-and-effect phenomena stemming from our having been slaves!

We, in our search for our identity, have declared ourselves Afro Descendants. It is our identity which was taken, and it is the lack our identity which is a constant source of anger and despair today. Because we lack our identity we have suffered the denial by history of many of our rights. Economically and developmentally we are currently suffering the aftermath of what took place during slavery.

The UN has noted that some States have taken the initiative to apologize and have paid reparation, where appropriate, for grave and massive human rights violations. Afro Descendants have had our mother tongue, culture and religion forcibly removed: hence, our loss of identity and the negation of our essence. We Afro Descendants have not existed in the United Nations system. Therefore our prayer is for official recognition of our self-chosen collective identity and reparations.

Since racial discrimination is found in the "negation of the essence of the victims," this is our proposal for the elimination of racial discrimination.

Mr. Silis Muhammad

Written and Oral Statements to the UN in 2001

Statements delivered in 2001 were heard and responded to by the UN. Oral statements were delivered by Mr. Silis Muhammad unless otherwise noted.

Documents of 2001 in order of presentation:

1. Written Statement to the Commission on Human Rights, April 2001

2. Oral Statement to the Commission on Human Rights

3. Oral Statement to the Working Group on Minorities, May 2001

4. Oral Statement of Attorney Harriett AbuBakr to the Working Group on Minorities

5. Written Statement to the Sub-Commission on the Promotion and Protection of Human Rights, August 2001

6. Oral Statement to the Sub-Commission on the Promotion and Protection of Human Rights

1) Written Statement to the 57th Session of the Commission on Human Rights

Provisional Agenda item 14, Specific Groups and Individuals (b) Minorities

During this 57th session of the Commission on Human Rights, Mr. Silis Muhammad will speak on behalf of so-called African-Americans for the ninth time. He has been bringing their collective prayer to the UN because the lingering effects of plantation slavery have left them in a deprived state. They are deprived of their original identity. They have experienced the forcible removal of culture, religion and 'mother tongue'. The annihilation of their 'mother tongue' is the extermination of their identity.

African-Americans in North, Central and South America and throughout the Diaspora all suffer from the loss of their identity. They did not come to the Americas willingly and they did not come as English speaking Christians with an Anglo-American culture. Neither did they come as Christians speaking Spanish or Portuguese or enjoying Spanish or Portuguese culture. Forcibly displaced from their common territory and scattered throughout the Americas Region and beyond, they have never questioned that they belong to each other as a group. Yet they have been denied the human rights that other groups enjoy: the right to speak their own language, practice their own religion and enjoy their own culture. Thus they are dispossessed of those human rights possessed by every minority and People and protected by the United Nations. They have not been in possession of their human rights for the past 400 years.

Although they are a People, and not a minority, African-Americans in the United States are placed within a minority status, as every scholar knows. The problems encountered in bringing the gravity of their position to light are extreme because the destruction of their identity has been hidden behind the U.S. Government's "melting pot" image. African-Americans mimic the identity of the majority. They are buried and hidden within the majority language, religion and culture, so very much so that United Nations in making its laws has left them out, it seems: it is not known immediately where they fit. To be left out of both the Declaration on the Rights of Minorities, and the International Covenant on Civil and Political Rights, is to not have political recognition of their human rights.

African-Americans support the notion that "Race" is a constituent element of the definition of minority. For more than 400 years they have been mindful, daily, of a consciousness of "otherness", with respect to racial differences. Unlike the Indigenous Peoples who were native to the territory, before colonization, and who formed many groups and spoke several languages, African-Americans were displaced from their common territory, and yet they invoke their similar characteristics in order to obtain their rights. Since the African-American "Racial" group is a group destroyed, it is axiomatic knowledge that they are a different racial group from the majority: they have neither racial dignity nor political bond.

Since collectively, they enjoy no political recognition, one might wonder how a complaint can be brought under international law. When they are able to argue about a violation of their human rights, and they should now be able in that they are racial members of the human family, this is their complaint: we are human beings, but to this date and time we are denied the human right of speaking our 'mother tongue' in violation of Article 27 of the International

Covenant on Civil and Political Rights, which the United States of America has ratified.

Today the U.S. Government makes itself responsible for the rights of minorities within its jurisdiction to speak their 'mother tongue' in community with other members of their group. African-Americans cannot speak theirs. While the U.S. may assert that African-Americans are deprived of the use of their mother tongue, and not denied its use, scholars will agree that the very act of taking their 'mother tongue' away was for the express purpose of denying them the use of it. In fact, the act is tantamount to a permanent ongoing denial. Since their 'mother tongue' is taken away, they are both deprived and denied the use of it. And in its place, the U.S. continually has forced its Anglo-Saxon 'mother tongue' upon them for the past 400 years. Absent their 'mother tongue', they become a non-People, living without a permanent identity.

The African-American experience is an example for the civilized world of a holocaust wherein identity is forcibly and perpetually exterminated. Throughout their history, the U.S. Government, for the benefit of the white majority, perpetuated the crime by systematically obstructing their attempts to identify and bring dignity to themselves. The international community well understands that human dignity is attached to identity. African-Americans in the U.S. have cried out in many ways over many years for the restoration of their dignity as a people, yet their cry has been manipulated by the acts of the U.S. Government.

In the 1950s and '60s African-Americans by the hundreds of thousands joined and built the Lost-Found Nation of Islam, which was the most successful autonomy model for slave descendants in the U.S. During the same time period, the U.S. Government demonstrated its opposition to their rising consciousness in many ways, including its counter-intelligence program. Ultimately the U.S. Government used its media, its laws and its military to promote integration. As the international community knows, the integration and civil rights movement caused African-Americans to believe that they might one day achieve equality. Now they are beginning to understand that as long as they are forced to assume the identity of the ruling culture, they are placed in an underling position from which there is no escape.

Today the integration movement is viewed by experts as having brought about the demise of an independent Black economy and the weakening of the Black family and Black community. With their cohesiveness thus disrupted, the U.S. Government is now firmly in the position of being able to manipulate the African-American choice of leaders at the most crucial time in their rise.

There has never been a more grave situation for African-Americans and the United States of America. From the grass-root to the intellectual elite, they are coming into awareness that the U.S. Government has never intended or acted to do justice toward the descendants of its slaves. They are realizing that the lingering effects of slavery are intentionally placed to keep them in a permanent underling position. They are rising with this knowledge, and moving toward a mass cry for reparation. Concurrently, the potential for U.S. Government manipulation of African-Americans through media appointed leaders is at its highest point. If the African-American people see their upward movement being turned against them once again, violent racial confrontation is assured.

Once again, Mr. Silis Muhammad is delivering to the Commission on Human Rights a recommendation on behalf of African-Americans. He asks for United Nations expert and technical assistance in the establishment of an inclusive forum of African-American leaders. This forum would serve as the decision making and negotiating body for African-Americans in their dealings with the U.S. Government. The forum would also serve as a model for African-Americans in the Americas and throughout the Diaspora. It would provide a protected environment wherein the gravity of the current situation can be examined and the extent of damages can be determined. Within such a forum Black leaders from the grass-root, the community organizations, religious organizations, professional organizations as well as scholars, business leaders and politicians, can discuss and conclude on the means of reparation most beneficial to the restoration of African-Americans individually and as a People.

In conclusion, United Nations intervention is urgently called for in the restoration of the human rights and collective political identity of African-Americans. UN intervention is urgently called for as well, to protect and assist African-American leaders within a forum, as they seek to determine the damage they have sustained and the means of reparation needed in order to bring them back to life as a People.

2) Oral Statement to the 57th Session of the Commission on Human Rights

14. Specific Groups and Individuals: (b) Minorities

Greetings, Mr. Chairman. I have come to the UN, from the United States, where stands the Statue of Liberty. I do not say statue of Liberty in mockery. Liberty is an important word to me, and I hope it has a meaning to each and every one of you.

We, African Americans, were, and are still mentally, politically and economically deprived, as every scholar knows. We were captured in slavery. My question is, do we now fit in the category of minority, or national minority or a people? Four hundred years of plantation slavery and its lingering effects have left us deprived and denied the use of our 'mother tongue', and thus, OUTSIDE OF a definite place within the UN system.

We are all from a common a territory, Africa, and from many tribes who spoke many languages. Like the Indigenous Americans, who were colonized and are <u>receiving recognition as peoples, and reparations</u>, we recognize ourselves as a "race" of people, by virtue of our origin and other commonalties and traits: the sufferance of slavery and its legacies, and the feeling of difference (or otherness) from the majority. We are not in control of our intellectual future, or our political and economic future. It would be impossible for the United States to implement a prayer for the reconstruction of our 'mother tongue', <u>owing to forced breeding between slaves</u>. We are without a definite identity, as to tribe, nation or people.

The international community does well understand that human dignity is attached to identity. We African Americans do not know where we fit. And what is more, I have learned, the United Nations does not know where we fit.

To this date and time we are denied, and deprived, the human right of speaking our 'mother tongue' in violation of Article 27 of the International Covenant on Civil and Political Rights, which the U.S. has ratified. Therefore, our prayer is for reparations, for the damage suffered, during this <u>ongoing</u> legal, and moral <u>wrong</u>. We ask that the Commission on Human Rights hear us as we demand our choice of reconstituting ourselves. May the Commission on Human Rights find a category within which we fit, or make a category in which we will fit? For the acts of wrong that the U.S. Government has committed against the very character of the UN -- HUMAN RIGHTS for everyone, everywhere -- we recommend a reparations sanction.

3) Working Group on Minorities, Seventh Session, 14-18 May 2001

Agenda Item 3 (b)

Examining possible solutions to problems involving minorities, including the promotion of mutual understanding between and among minorities and Governments

If I could express a feeling in words, and that is difficult to do, I would like to say thank you to the Chairperson, Mr. Eide, Mr. Bengoa, and other members of the Working Group for their guidance, and for being dutiful to their profession.

The United Nations does not recognize us, the African American people in the United States, or know where we fit, I have seen. Four hundred years of plantation slavery and its lingering effects have left us deprived of and denied our 'mother tongue', and thus, outside of a definite place within the UN system, in violation of Article 27 of the ICCPR. This is an ongoing wrong. It is our prayer that the Working Group on Minorities will eventually recognize us, for we do recognize ourselves as the African American people, internally.

We are all from a common territory, Africa, and from many tribes who spoke many languages. Like the Indigenous Americans, who were colonized and are receiving recognition as peoples, and reparations, we recognize ourselves as a "race" of people, by virtue of our common origin, the sufferance of slavery and its legacies, and the wrongful act of forced breeding between the slaves which produced a changed African American people. Thus we are without a recognized identity as to tribe, nation or a people, and we are not in control of our future.

We are a people experiencing, in reality, the process of ethnogenesis. We ask that the Working Group on Minorities let us know what it recommends in relation to our desire to reconstruct our lost ties and reconstitute ourselves, since there are at present no international instruments, arbitrations, mechanisms or laws requiring the recognition of minorities that can restrain ethnic conflict.

4) Statement of Attorney Harriett AbuBakr

To the Working Group on Minorities, Seventh Session, 14-18 May 2001

Agenda Item 3 (b) Examining possible solutions to problems involving minorities, including the promotion of mutual understanding between and among minorities and Governments

Greetings Mr. Chairman, Members of the Working Group on Minorities. My name is Harriett AbuBakr. I am an attorney at law, and founding member of the National Commission for Reparations, an organization representing African Americans in the United States. For several years I have come here to speak on the particular problems of African Americans. The response of the Working Group to African American issues has been steadfast, and it has given me confidence in your guidance. This year I will attempt to place my remarks within the broad theme that you have given us, the right to effective participation of minorities in the society of which they form a part.

We African Americans, whose ancestors were taken captive and enslaved, are a new people, and a new family among the families of man. Amongst ourselves we are keenly aware of our kinship and our difference from others, including even the Africans from whose arms we were torn. Today we are a part of a society established by those who captured and enslaved our ancestors.

During slavery we were forcibly removed from our mother tongue, culture and religion, and cruelly subjected to forced mixed breeding. We cannot look upon ourselves today and say "I am this or I am that." The painful truth is that we do not know ourselves. Forged in the most terrible of human experiences, that of being stripped of our very humanity, we have risen with the sure knowledge of one thing: we are human beings and we are entitled to know ourselves, to be ourselves and to enjoy human rights.

As a new people, our call for reparation is motivated by a profound desire for justice in human society. Our first concern is with our own restoration as a people. To be restored, we must form a foundation upon which to manifest our human spirit, new and changed as it is. We want our will for our future generations to be made manifest in the society in which we live. How can this occur?

We have no place in the Constitution of the United States. It is a document which to this day defines us as 3/5 of a human being. How can we effectively participate in a society where such a constitution is held sacred? Most of us believe the majority citizens would rather go to war with us than break down and rebuild their constitution in order to make it include our living will and protect us with the law that arises out of it.

Reparations for us must involve restoration of our human rights. In order to effectively participate in the society in which we live, we feel we must have some appropriate degree of autonomy, otherwise the insult to our human spirit that we are forced to endure daily will continue to erupt in physical violence, such as the widespread rioting that shut down Cincinnati approximately one month ago.

We continue to call for the expert guidance of the Working Group on Minorities in order to find the way through this delicate time in our resurrection. In the United States we are among those leading the African American people into an understanding of what has happened to them. The cry for justice and reparation is arising in us as if from the bottom of a deep well. With your assistance we must make sure that it leads to our restoration.

The needs of people are the reason for the development of law. We ask, will the Working Group on Minorities go to the farthest extent of its mandate in order to cause minority protection to develop in accord with our needs? Thank you for your attention.

5) Written Statement to the 53rd Session of the

Sub-Commission on the Promotion and Protection of Human Rights

Agenda item 5. Prevention of discrimination and protection of indigenous peoples and minorities

The following statement is offered by Mr. Silis Muhammad on behalf of the African American people.

We know that the United Nations does not recognize us, the African American people. Four hundred years of plantation slavery and its lingering effects have left us deprived of and denied our 'mother tongue', and thus outside of a definite place within the UN system. Although we are a people, and not a minority, in the United States we are placed within a minority status. We mimic the identity of the majority. We are buried and hidden within the majority language, culture and religion so very much that the United Nations in making its laws has left us out, it seems: it is not known immediately where we fit. This is an ongoing wrong. Throughout the Americas Region and beyond we are a people numbering 240,000,000, yet we live as if lost, without a recognized identity and without our human rights.

Since 1997 we have been delivering written and oral statements to the Sub-Commission on the Promotion and Protection of Human Rights. We have informed the Sub-Commission that we, the African American people, have been denied the human rights that other groups enjoy, as protected by Article 27 of the International Covenant on Civil and Political Rights, which the U.S. Government has ratified. We have told the Sub-Commission how we suffer from having been denied and deprived of our original language, our original culture and our original religion. We have told the

Sub-Commission that we have been in this condition, living without our identity for the past 400 years

We have informed the Sub-Commission that the U.S. Government has systematically obstructed our attempts to identify and bring dignity to ourselves. We have told the Sub-Commission that we want our international political identity restored, and as a result of the U.S. Government's acts against us, we require UN assistance. We have prayed to the Sub-Commission for specific assistance in our efforts to resurrect ourselves, and receive reparations and restoration of our human rights. Thus we are confident that the Sub-Commission is aware that human rights are not presently being enjoyed by the African American people.

We have also brought our prayers to the Working Group on Minorities: a working group of the Sub-Commission. This Working Group has been entrusted with the task of promoting the rights of minorities in accordance with the Declaration on the Rights of National, Ethnic, Religious and Linguistic Minorities. We thank the Sub-Commission for continuing to authorize the Working Group on Minorities, and support its efforts. We recognize that the Working Group on Minorities has made a consistent effort to respond to our prayers, and bring our issues to the Sub-Commission. We would like to thank the Working Group on Minorities, and urge the members, who are also members of this esteemed Sub-Commission, to steadfastly continue their efforts on our behalf.

It is our prayer that the Sub-Commission on the Promotion and Protection of Human Rights consider the following three recommendations to this, its 53rd Session:

We urgently recommend that the Sub-Commission place the African American people on its agenda, alongside indigenous peoples and minorities. By placing us on the agenda, the Sub-Commission would acknowledge that it recognizes us as a group: as we have never questioned that we belong to each other as a group. We ask the Sub-Commission to take the bold step of beginning the official UN recognition of us by placing us on its agenda. We also asked to be placed on the agenda so that the experts of the Sub-Commission may be able to consider our issues and make decisions and offer resolutions on our behalf.

We recommend that the Sub-Commission invite the Working Group on Minorities to present before it a Working Paper of the Working Group on Minorities entitled *Existence and Recognition of Minorities*, document E/CN.4/Sub.2/AC.5/2000/WP.2, written by Sub-Commissioner Mr. Jose Bengoa. We believe that presentation and discussion of this working paper will benefit the Sub-Commission by offering some alternatives to the present understanding of the situation of the African American people in the United States and throughout the Region of the Americas.

In regard to the mass cry for reparation of the African American people, which the UN is confronting at the upcoming World Conference Against Racism, we ask the Sub-Commission to put forward a specific recommendation. We ask the Sub-Commission to recommend that UN expert and technical assistance be granted in the establishment of an inclusive forum of African American leaders from the U.S.: a forum which would serve as a model for the Americas Region. This forum would seek to determine the damage we have sustained and the means of reparation needed in order to bring about our resurrection and restoration. It would also serve as a negotiating body for the African American people in their dealings with the U.S. Government. Without UN protection, there will be dangerous potential for U.S. Government manipulation of this mass movement, as there has been with mass movements of our people in the past.

6) Sub-Commission on the Promotion and Protection of Human Rights

Oral intervention under agenda item 5:

Prevention of discrimination and protection of indigenous peoples and minorities

We recommend a forum for the African American people, who are descendants of slaves, throughout North America, Central America, South America and the Diaspora. We recommend that a trust fund be established for activities under this forum.

We did not come to the Americas willingly, and we did not come as Christians, speaking English, Spanish or Portuguese. We are all from a common territory, Africa, yet we are from many tribes who spoke many languages. The Indigenous Americans who spoke languages, and who were colonized, are now receiving reparations and recognition as peoples. We, likewise, recognize ourselves as a "race" of people, by virtue of our common origin, the sufferance of slavery and its legacies, and the wrongful act of forced breeding between slave and the slave masters. This forced breeding produced a changed African people approximately 240,000,000 strong, living the Americas Region, and lost from our identity. Thus we are without any UN recognized identity.

We urgently recommend that the Sub-Commission place the African American people on its agenda, alongside indigenous peoples and minorities. We have never questioned that we belong to each other as a group. By placing us on the agenda the Sub-Commission would then be able to consider our issues, including where we fit. At the very least, we are another category of people; but presently, we have no recognized UN Human Rights.

Oral Statements to Regional Seminars for Afrodescendants

Statements delivered to Regional Seminars on Afrodescendants in 2001 and 2002 were heard and responded to by the UN.

Oral Statements to Regional Seminars on Afrodescendants in order of presentation:

1. Statement to the Regional Seminar in La Ceiba, Honduras, March 2002

2. Statement to the First Informal Workshop on Afrodescendants in Geneva, Switzerland, Morning Session, May 2001

3. Statement to the First Informal Workshop on Afrodescendants, Afternoon Session

1) The Regional Seminar on Afro-Descendants in the Americas

La Ceiba, Honduras, 21 to 24 March, 2002

There would be no racial discrimination against us if we, the so-called African Americans, had not been dispossessed of our homeland, Africa, taken into slavery for 430 years and stripped of our identity: mother tongue, culture and religion.

We descendants, in South America, Central America, North America and throughout the Diaspora, are suffering the lingering effects of slavery.

The taking away of one's identity has the same effect as does racial discrimination: it places the powerful in rulership over the powerless. Call it what you will, discrimination against us is born out of the loss of identity. Still today the Black man is denied the means of getting up, or reclaiming his lost ties: his identity. When he tries he faces opposition.

For the lack of knowing his original family name, the Black man accepts a family name that fits the region where he resides. You see the difficulty that we have in communicating with each other. We are of the same family, you and I, yet we sit across the table speaking these European languages: English, Spanish and Portuguese. The slave masters forced these languages upon our foreparents. They are not our languages.

Once, long ago, our freedom to think and speak in our own languages was willfully taken. The door to our identity was permanently shut! This door must be opened! During slavery our mother tongue, culture and religion were mercilessly destroyed. Consider the magnitude of the damage that this did to us. Reparations in the form of money alone will not repair this! Complete restoration should be our demand. Let's give ourselves a name and begin it.

The Durban Conference Against Racial Discrimination has asked the Commission on Human Rights to establish a working group or mechanism in order to deal with the issues of the Afrodescendants' communities. The door is now open in the United Nations! Come, let's grasp this opportunity! Lets go there with a name for ourselves, that we have chosen, together, and tell them that we want a place in the UN system, collectively. We are a family. This is our chance to reclaim ourselves, or our identity. Quoting professor Bengoa, the process of reclaiming lost ties is called "ethnogenesis."

Like the Indigenous Peoples, we are many diverse peoples and nations. We do not have to give up our diversity, or our leadership to become as one, politically. The Indigenous Peoples are even more diverse than we, yet they have been able to come together under one name in order to gain human rights protection, reparations and restoration. They have a place in the UN system. We do not. Cannot we do the same as they, or better? We are 250,000,000 strong, approximately. Given a platform, 250 million people have a lot of political power. We need a name. I offer, the name LOST FOUND Peoples, to begin the discussion. There is no question that we were lost, and that Professor Jose Bengoa and the Working Group on Minorities are in the process of trying to help us find a place where we fit.

Silis Muhammad.

Editor's Note: The name Lost-Found Peoples was not accepted, and the name Afrodescendants was agreed upon by unanimous consent.

2) Informal Workshop on Afro-descendants in the Americas

Working Group on Minorities

Morning Session

May 19, 2001

Statement by Mr. Silis Muhammad

Greetings Mr. Chairman, members of the Working Group on Minorities. I would like to thank each one of you for your part in organizing this special informal workshop for Afro-Descendants in the Americas. Also, I thank the NGOs that contributed to organizing this workshop.

My name is Silis Muhammad. For four years I have been attending the meetings of the Working Group on Minorities to deliver prayers on behalf of African Americans in the United States. From my first intervention before this esteemed group of experts, my concern has been with the subject of today's Agenda Item 2: The relevance of minority protection to the Afro-Americans, and its relation to the Declaration on the Rights of Persons Belonging to National or Ethnic, Religious and Linguistic Minorities.

When we African Americans consider the Declaration on the Rights of Minorities, we conclude that we remain a lost people. While we are a people and not a minority, in the United States we are placed within a minority status. Thus, the U.S. Government, with knowledge that it has denied us our identity for the past 400 years, is in violation of the aforementioned Declaration. In Article 2 the Declaration emphasizes that minorities have the right to enjoy their culture and identity.

In our first intervention before this group we questioned whether the so-called African Americans are in possession of their human rights. We concluded that the UN does not recognize us, or know where we fit. Four hundred years of plantation slavery and its lingering effects have left us outside of a definite place within the UN system, and thus not in possession of our human rights. Today we thank the Working

Group on Minorities for demonstrating its willingness to hear our concerns and assist us.

We know that to the extent that we have been deprived of our culture, our religion and our language, we do not have human rights. During the period we were enslaved, we lost our identity: our 'mother tongue', our culture and religion – by whatever names they were then called. Owing to the acts of plantation slavery and its lingering effects, we have been <u>duplicated</u> as a type of clone of the Anglo-Saxon: we speak their English, practice their religion, and have lived their culture. In addition, the wrongful act of forced breeding between the slaves has produced a changed African American people. Thus we are without a definite identity as to tribe, nation or a people, and we are not in control of our future.

African Americans in North, Central and South America and throughout the Diaspora all suffer from the loss of their identity. We did not come to the Americas willingly and we did not come as English speaking Christians with an Anglo-American culture. Neither did we come as Spanish or Portuguese speaking Christians with Spanish or Portuguese influenced culture. African Americans are a people who for more than 400 years have been mindful, daily, of a consciousness of "otherness", with respect to racial differences. We have been forcibly displaced from our common territory and scattered throughout the Americas Region and beyond. The African American "racial" group is a group destroyed, having neither racial dignity nor political bond.

We African Americans in the United States have cried out in many ways over many years for the restoration of our dignity as a people. Yet the U.S. Government commits, daily, the international wrongful act of denying our existence while claiming respect for human rights. It is our desire to reconstitute ourselves, for we do recognize ourselves as the African American people, internally. It is also our desire to receive reparation from the U.S. Government for the ongoing loss of our 'mother tongue', and our internationally recognized political identity. We ask that the Working Group on Minorities let us know what it recommends in relation to our desire to reconstitute ourselves, and to receive reparation and international political recognition.

In conclusion, it is our prayer that this body of experts, the Working Group on Minorities, will become the force within the United Nations for the creation of international instruments, arbitration mechanisms and laws that require States to recognize and respect the dignity of the minorities and peoples under their jurisdiction.

3) Informal Workshop on Afro-descendants in the Americas

Working Group on Minorities

Afternoon Session

May 19, 2001

Statement by Mr. Silis Muhammad

Read by Harriett AbuBakr

For the past three years I have been asking the UN to provide the forum for African American leaders, and this they did.

This forum was the closest they could come. I want to thank Mr. Eide, Mr. Bengoa, Mr. Sik Yuen and their experts for giving up their Saturday to sit down with the African American leaders and try to <u>find a place within the existing UN declarations and covenants</u> where we can fit.

We could take another 100 years and create another wheel, but a wheel exists already and all we have to do is step within it. They are here - the expert and technical support - to help us step within the wheel. They recognize that we are all from Africa and that we call ourselves African Americans and Afrodescendants.

Professor Bengoa wrote a working paper that was approved by the Working Group, discussing whether to make race an element of the definition of minority, and discussing whether we should be recognized as a people. Did you read it? Are we not a race, and do we not have a feeling of otherness from those in power because we lost our 'mother tongue', religion and culture when we were brought into slavery?

Forced mixed breeding renders us human but without human rights. Latin Americans, Central Americans and Black Americans in the United States and Canada do not have their human rights. While you are talking about marginalization, discrimination, autonomy - you first need collective human rights and political recognition. That's why these UN experts are here.

Written and Oral Statements to the World Conference Against Racism

Statements delivered in 2001 were heard and responded to by the UN.

Documents presented to the World Conference Against Racism in order of presentation:

1) Oral Statement of Mr. Silis Muhammad to the Plenary Session of the World Conference Against Racism in Durban, South Africa, September 2001

1) Written Statement to the World Conference Against Racism, Racial Discrimination, Xenophobia and Related Intolerance, 2001

1) World Conference Against Racism, Racial Discrimination,

Xenophobia and Related Intolerance

Oral intervention under provisional agenda theme 5:

Provision of effective remedies, recourse, redress, (compensatory) and other measures

at the national, regional and international level

We recommend a forum for the African American people: those who, due to our merciful parents, are the descendants of slaves, throughout North America, Central and South America, and the Diaspora. We recommend that a trust fund be established for activities under this forum, funded by all governments in which we are domiciled, or by any government or person[s] sympathetic to our quest for human rights.

We did not come to the Americas willingly, and we did not come as Christians, speaking English, Spanish, Portuguese or French. We are all from a common territory, Africa, where we are from many tribes who spoke many languages. The Indigenous Americans, who spoke many languages, and who were colonized, are now receiving reparations and should be receiving full recognition as peoples. We African Americans want to be restored, and recognized, and this is a form of reparations which can be examined and defined more completely in a forum. We are lost from our origins in Africa. Four hundred years of slavery, coupled with forced breeding between slaves and the slave masters, produced a people who have lost more than their independent character. It produced a people whose children are lost from their identity: mother tongue, religion and culture. We African Americans, who are the victims of slavery, will not mortgage the future of our generations to come.

For the past four years the UN Working Group on Minorities has been hard at work to find out where we fit, and to help us obtain a UN recognized identity. If my humble opinion may serve any use, let the name which identifies African Americans in the UN be "LOST FOUND Peoples." There is no question that we were lost, and that the Working Group on Minorities has been trying to find a place where we fit.

We urgently recommend that the World Conference Against Racism declare a decade to consider our issues, including whether "LOST FOUND Peoples" is the term that best identifies us: as at present, we have no UN collective human rights.

2) Written Statement to the World Conference Against Racism,

Racial Discrimination, Xenophobia and Related Intolerance

All For Reparations and Emancipation (AFRE)

Recommendations to the WCAR on the Issue of Reparations

All For Reparations and Emancipation would like to offer recommendations to the World Conference Against Racism, Racial Discrimination, Xenophobia and Related Intolerance

on the issue of reparations as it concerns African-Americans in the U.S. We hope that the World Conference will deem our recommendations worthy of consideration. We are especially hopeful that our recommendation for an inclusive forum for African-Americans (recommendation number three) might be recognized as a peaceful and progressive method of examining the gravity of the lingering effects of slavery, and of examining reparations as a remedy from the victim's viewpoint.

Our organization's leader, Mr. Silis Muhammad, has a long and respected history of African-American grass-root leadership. In 1994, after years of reparations advocacy, he delivered to the United Nations a petition for reparations for African-Americans under Communications Procedure 1503. Since that time he has intervened frequently at the Commission on Human Rights, the Sub-Commission on the Promotion and Protection of Human Rights and the Working Group on Minorities. His issue has been the destruction of the identity of African-Americans, and the resulting fact that African-Americans, collectively, have no human rights. The problems encountered in bringing the gravity of the legacies of plantation slavery to light are extreme because the destruction of identity of African-Americans in the U.S. has been hidden behind the government's "melting pot" image.

African-Americans did not come to America willingly, and they did not come as English speaking Christians, with an Anglo-Saxon culture. African-Americans are a people who for more than 400 years have never questioned that they belong to each other as a group, and yet they have been denied the human rights that other groups enjoy: the right to speak their own language, practice their own religion and enjoy their own culture.

The African-American experience is an example for the civilized world of a holocaust wherein identity is forcibly and perpetually exterminated. With the denial of the 'mother tongue', the slaves were severed from their identity. Throughout their history, the U.S. Government, for the benefit of the white majority, perpetuated the denial by systematically obstructing the attempts of African-Americans to identify themselves. The international community well understands that human dignity is attached to identity. African-Americans in the U.S. have cried out in many ways over many years for the restoration of their dignity as a people, yet their cry has been manipulated by the acts of the U.S. Government. Having been forced to assume the identity of the ruling culture, they are placed in an underling position from which there is no escape. How can they escape from a prison that many cannot even see? Only racism can be seen, and that is but a symptom of the prison. African-Americans are in a grave situation. They need assistance from the United Nations.

Since collectively, African-Americans enjoy no international recognition, one might wonder how charges can be brought under international law to substantiate the claim for reparations. Silis Muhammad has stated, "When we are able to argue about a violation of our human rights, this is our complaint: we are human beings, but to this date and time we are denied the human right of speaking our 'mother tongue' in violation of Article 27 of the International Covenant on Civil and Political Rights, which the United States of America has ratified."

Silis Muhammad is among the first, if not the first, to bring the issue of African-American reparations to the United Nations, and be heard. He has been consistently intervening before the human rights bodies with arguments on the legal implications of the lingering effects of plantation slavery. The position of AFRE is that we would not look favorably upon an offer of reparations that did not include restoration of collective human rights and international political recognition of African-Americans. It is for this reason that we make the following recommendations to the World Conference Against Racism:

1. We recommend that the World Conference pass a resolution declaring the lingering effects of plantation slavery

a crime as related to 'mother tongue'. Such a resolution would affirm that the act of denying the slaves the right to speak the 'mother tongue' is tantamount to a permanent ongoing denial for which there is no remedy.

2. We recommend that the World Conference urge the General Assembly to declare a UN decade to examine, in depth, the lingering effects of plantation slavery in the Americas.

3. We recommend that the World Conference encourage the Office of the High Commissioner for Human Rights to offer UN expert and technical assistance in the organization of an inclusive forum for African-American leaders. The forum would provide an environment wherein the gravity of the current situation can be examined and the extent of damages can be determined. Within such a forum, the victims can discuss and conclude on the means of reparation most beneficial to their restoration individually and as a People.

4. We recommend that the World Conference encourage the governments concerned to voluntarily and immediately establish tax exempt status for slave descendants; a status which will be in effect until both reparations and restoration of human rights have been achieved.

Written and Oral Statements to the UN in 2000

Statements delivered in 2000 were heard and responded to by the UN. Statements were delivered by Mr. Silis Muhammad unless otherwise noted.

1. Written Statement to the Commission on Human Rights, April 2000

2. Oral Statement to the Commission on Human Rights

3. Oral Statement to the Working Group on Minorities, May 2000

4. Oral Statement of Attorney Harriett AbuBakr to the Working Group on Minorities

5. Oral Statement of Ida Hakim to the Working Group on Minorities

6. Written Statement to the Sub-Commission on the Promotion and Protection of Human Rights, August 2000

7. Oral Statement to the Sub-Commission on the Promotion and Protection of Human Rights

1) Written Statement to the 56th Session of the Commission on Human Rights

Provisional Agenda Item 14. Specific groups and individuals: (b) Minorities.

1. Silis Muhammad is the spiritual son of the Honorable Elijah Muhammad. He sojourns amid forty million Black men and women in the United States of America whose foreparents were brought to the United States aboard slave ships. They were brought to America over 400 years ago. During the period of plantation slavery, were forcibly denied the right of speaking their 'mother tongue'.

2. Today, the lingering effects of plantation slavery deny us, the so-called African-Americans, the enjoyment of speaking our 'mother tongue' in community with other members of our group. This inherent human right is set forth in Article 27 of the International Covenant on Civil and Political Rights. We, the so-called African-Americans, are charging the United States of America with the "denial" of the use of our 'mother tongue'.

3. Article 27 of the International Covenant on Civil and Political Rights states, "In those States in which ethnic, religious or linguistic minorities exist, persons belonging to such minorities shall not be denied the right, in community with other members of their group, to enjoy their own culture, to profess and practice their own religion, or to use their own language."

4. We are human beings, but to this date and time we are denied the human right of speaking our 'mother tongue': it was taken during slavery. The United States grants the right today for us to speak it. Then speak it, one might say. How

can we speak what the U.S. has denied us the use of? If our 'mother tongue' is taken away, aren't we denied the use of it? No! One may say, you are deprived the use of it; there is a difference. Is not to be deprived of the use of our 'mother tongue' the same as being denied the use of it? No! Says the State, to be denied the use of it presupposes it is in your possession; while being deprived of its use presupposes it has been taken away. Well, since it has been taken away, we are both deprived and denied the use of it. The very act of taking our 'mother tongue' away was for the express purpose of denying us the use of it. In fact, the act is tantamount to a gross and excessive permanent denial. The United States craved for the denial of our use of it so strongly that it deprived us of the very instrument.

5. Thus, this will be viewed as a gross and an excessive act of denial of the United States to permit the so-called African-Americas to speak their 'mother tongue' in community with other members of their group. While the act of the United States may be viewed as an act against humanity, equally so has the United States made itself responsible for the rights of minorities, within its jurisdiction, to not be denied the use of their own language, in community with other members of their group. We, the so-called African-American, cannot speak ours. The United States grossly denies us the right, having deprived us, continually, of the very instrument. And in its place, the United States continually has forced its Anglo-Saxon 'mother tongue' upon us for the past four hundred years. Absent our 'mother tongue', we are a non-people: living in a state of civil death.

6. In addition, we are denied a permanent identity. Rent from our land in Africa, our roots, sold and forced into slavery: we have been recognized as slaves, Niggers, Negroes, Coloreds, Black-Americans and today we are the so-called African

Americans. While holding us in this ever-revolving state, the United States holds itself out as being in full compliance with Article 27 of the International Covenant on Civil and Political Rights. Yet the United States causes us to remain trapped within the Anglo-American culture regenerating its 'mother tongue', in reality, its identity. One's 'mother tongue' is the essential route to one's identity. It is the manner in which one's identity is passed from generation to generation and through which one's culture and religion flow.

7. Professor Gulillame Siemienski's working paper on "Education rights of minorities: Hague Recommendations", states that language, but not just any language, one's 'mother tongue' is intimately bound with identity. Absent exposure to our original tongue at the earliest possible stages in life and in primary and secondary levels of schooling, how could and can we speak it with other members of our community and preserve our individual identity? By forcibly stripping us of the use of our language and of the right to be educated in the same, the Government of the United States deracinated our collective identity, making our condition irreversible. We need special assistance.

8. While we are a People, and not a minority, in the United States we are placed within a minority status. Hence we call upon the United Nations to come to our succor under Article 27 of the International Covenant on Civil and Political Rights, as the lingering annihilation of our 'mother tongue' and the continual force, by the United States, imposed upon us to speak its Anglo-Saxon 'mother tongue' at the earliest possible stages in our lives, is the continual extermination of both our individual and collective identity. Absent identity we do not have our own culture, absent culture we live, today, in a state of ongoing civil death: genocide. We are a people who are buried, politically. The United States has killed our human

rights and has covered us over with its own, fraudulently, by trick and by duress. We were buried and hidden, so very much so, the United Nations in making its laws has left us out, it seems: it is not known immediately where we fit. In the United States, we, the so-called African-Americans, mimic the human rights of the majority; but in reality, we are in the position of a minority, as every scholar knows.

9. In conclusion, we pray for compensation in the form of reparations. We ask that the United States pay reparations to the so-called African Americans, since the United States cannot restore our 'mother tongue' if ever it wanted to. Nor can the United States continue, illegally, to choose and force one upon us, which it has done for the last 400 years. The United States should be held liable, at least, for the last 51 years, plus the additional years which are needed to resolve this issue. We ask that the United Nations place this reparation sanction upon America if the identity and language of minorities and Peoples are to be preserved. The precise dollar amount will not herein be stated, but will be presented when we are satisfied that the gravity of our argument, in the eyes of the United Nations, warrants it. Along with a dollar amount, we will ask for the release of a number of African-American human rights victims who have been unjustly incarcerated in federal and state penitentiaries. Finally, we ask that the United Nations impose a sanction on the United States in the form of exemption of all taxation upon our people for as long as this issue is in the hands of the United Nations.

2) Oral Statement to the Commission on Human Rights

Item 14 (b) Specific Groups and Individuals: Minorities

The lingering effects of plantation slavery leave my people and me in a deprived state. We are deprived of our 'mother tongue.' Today, the United States of America grants minorities the use of their own language. But mine was forcibly taken away. I am denied and deprived of its use.

Article 27 of the International Covenant on Civil and Political Rights, which the United States has ratified, declares, "In those States in which ethnic, religious or linguistic minorities exist, persons belonging to such minorities shall not be denied the right, in community with other members of their group, to enjoy their own culture, to profess and practice their own religion, or to use their own language.

We, the so-called African-Americans, in the aftermath of plantation slavery, cannot speak our own language, in community with other members of our group. The U.S. Government took it away.

African-Americans originate from many parts of Africa encompassing hundreds of languages. Therefore, it would be impossible to implement the prayer of African-Americans regarding the loss of their 'mother tongue.' The inability to implement a remedy makes it impossible to enforce any law. Our prayer, however, is for reparations. In this way America can address this legal and moral wrong: we will choose a language pleasing to us.

This argument is being made by a group that represents only one tenth of one percent of African-Americans in the United States. Nonetheless, the argument is made.

In conclusion, we ask that the United States pay reparations to the so-called African-Americans, as the United States cannot restore our 'mother tongue' if ever it wanted to. Nor should the United States continue, illegally, to choose and force one upon us, which it has done for the last 400 years. We ask that the Commission on Human Rights recommend a reparations sanction against the United States to ECOSOC and the General Assembly.

3) Oral Statement to the 6th session of the Working Group on Minorities, May 2000

Agenda Item 3 (b) to examine possible solutions to problems involving minorities

Greetings Mr. Chairman, members of the Working Group on Minorities.

The lingering effects of plantation slavery leave my people and me in a deprived state. We are deprived of our 'mother tongue'. To date, we are denied and deprived of its use.

Article 2.1 of the Declaration on the Rights of Persons Belonging to Minorities states: "Persons belonging to national or ethnic, religious and linguistic minorities have the right to enjoy their own culture, to profess and practice their own religion, and to use their own language, in private and in public, freely and without interference or any form of discrimination."

Today, the United States of America grants minorities the use of their own language. It has ratified Article 27, of the ICCPR, which declares: "In those States in which ethnic, religious or linguistic minorities exist, persons belonging to such minorities shall not be denied the right, in community with other members of their group, to enjoy their own culture, to profess and practice their own religion, or to use their own language."

But we, the so-called African-Americans, in the aftermath of plantation slavery, cannot speak our own language. The U.S. Government took it away: it was forcibly taken away.

African-Americans originate from many parts of Africa encompassing hundreds of languages. Therefore, it would be impossible to implement the prayer of African-Americans regarding the loss of their 'mother tongue'. The inability to implement a remedy makes it impossible to enforce any law. Our prayer is, however, for reparations. In this way America can address its legal wrong, and moral obligation. We will choose a language pleasing to us.

In conclusion, we ask that the Working Group on Minorities, in its report to the Sub-Commission, recommend that an expert be appointed to engage in dialogue with the U.S. Government. The urgent prayer of African-Americans for reparations should be the subject of this dialogue. Our recommendation is made in light of the fact that 40 million people are suffering this continuing legal wrong.

4) Sixth session of the Working Group on Minorities

Agenda Item 3(b) Examining possible solutions to problems involving minorities

Statement by Harriett AbuBakr

Greetings Mr. Chairman and members of the Working Group on Minorities,

I am grateful for the opportunity to speak a second time before the Working Group on Minorities. My name is Harriett AbuBakr. I am a descendant of slaves in the United States of America. I speak as an Attorney, and founding member of the National Commission for Reparations. My concern is with Agenda item 3 (b) examining possible solutions to problems involving minorities, and also Agenda item 3 (c) further measures for the protection of persons belonging to minorities which could act as examples or be replicated.

Article 1.1 of the Declaration on the Rights of Minorities says that, "States shall protect the existence and the national or ethnic, cultural, religious and linguistic identity of minorities within their respective territories and shall encourage conditions for the promotion of that identity."

Professor Edie in his commentary on the Declaration tells us that the first requirement of Article 1.1 is to protect the right to existence in its physical sense and the fourth requirement is to protect the identity. We African-Americans, from the 400-year experience of plantation slavery, know that physical existence has little value without identity. Therefore we are grateful that the Declaration on the Rights of Minorities recognizes the importance of identity.

Our experience is an example for the civilized world of a holocaust wherein identity is exterminated. Within our experience is the example of the means that a State can use to forcibly, intentionally and permanently sever a people from their identity. Within our experience is the example of how a people in such a deprived condition by their very nature, and against terrible opposition, will seek without rest to find their lost identity. Within our experience is the example of how a State systematically, for the benefit of the majority, can obstruct the attempts of a people to identify themselves. Within our experience is the example of what extraordinary damage can be sustained when a people's identity is lost and the identity of the majority is forced upon them.

Because of our experience with plantation slavery, we know how human dignity is attached to identity. We are a people, living within the United States as a minority. Without identity we have no legal/political status or recognition internationally, no respect from the majority population domestically, and no dignity among our fellow human beings.

We believe we can assist the Working Group on Minorities in defining the crime of destruction of identity and understanding its consequences upon civilization as a whole. Silis Muhammad refers to our current condition as civil death. We want to be restored from civil death so that we might live again in dignity, with respect. We believe we can help the Working Group on Minorities to develop measures that might serve as a solution for us and as an example for the civilized world.

African-Americans have been seeking an identity as a people since emancipation from slavery more than 100 years ago.

Since that time the majority population has called us niggers, negroes, colored, Black and African-American. They have forced upon us the Christian religion, the English language and the Anglo-American culture. Simultaneously, numbers of our people have searched far and wide trying to find an identity that would better fit our nature. Among the more prominent identities that we have claimed are Nubian Islamic Hebrews, Kemetic People, Hebrew Israelites, Moors, Israelite Lawkeepers, Kushites and Asiatic Blackmen and women. Politically our leaders have given us the United Negro Improvement Association, Simbionese Liberation Army, Pan African Nationalists, Black United Front, Afrikan People's Socialist Party, National Association for the Advancement of Colored People, Uhuru Movement, Black Panther Party for Self Defense, Republic of New Afrika, Black Radical Congress, New Black Panther Party and so on. Our leaders have borrowed from the cultures of other identities as well as inventing the Afrocentric and Rastafarian cultures. I am among those who have chosen the family of Shabazz, the religion of Islam and the Government and culture of the Lost Found Nation of Islam.

As you can see, we are fractured into many pieces as a people. We have searched and cried for collective identity while the U.S. Government has systematically sought to keep any of our leaders from gaining too much influence. The U.S. Government has defamed the best of our leaders and placed them in jail. While defaming or destroying our leaders, the U.S. Government has put forth leaders of its own choice through use of the media. The U.S. Government held us captive in plantation slavery, and it captures us still through manipulation, both of our will and of those who would help us around the world. Ours is a situation where conflict is certain if we are unable to bring an end to our captivity.

For some time Silis Muhammad has prayed that a forum for African-Americans be established at UN Headquarters. He has said that within a UN protected forum African-Americans can establish a council or governing body amongst themselves, and within this council they can begin the process of reclaiming or choosing our legal/political being and status as a people. Surely the Working Group on Minorities can now see the reason behind Mr. Muhammad's prayer.

Silis Muhammad has also prayed that the UN place a reparation sanction upon the United States. The demand for reparation is becoming widespread among African-Americans. UN involvement and protection is essential to us as we become ever more vulnerable to U.S. Government manipulation of our will.

I am here to ask the Working Group on Minorities to recognize us as a people and a minority in need of special assistance. We have suffered from the loss of that very thing the Declaration on the Rights of Minorities seeks to protect: identity. If our condition is not of concern to the UN, then how can the minorities and peoples of the earth find their protection in law that the UN creates? I am here to join Silis Muhammad in his prayer for the appointment of an expert to engage in dialogue with the United States on the subject of reparations. The National Commission for Reparations asks the Working Group on Minorities to consider his prayer and make a favorable recommendation to the Sub-Commission on behalf of so-called African-Americans.

Thank you Mr. Chairman.

5) Sixth session of the Working Group on Minorities

Agenda Item 4. The Future Role of the Working Group

Statement by Ida Hakim

Greetings Mr. Chairman and Members of the Working Group on Minorities. I appreciate being able to make a few comments. The sixth session of the Working Group has been greater than past sessions in my view. There is a serious working atmosphere and yet a relaxed atmosphere. It seems that the Minorities themselves are being given more consideration and that is much appreciated. Also, the working papers are found to be very informative and beneficial. The attendance of more State representatives is gratefully noted.

In my view the intent of the Working Group to promote mutual understanding between and among minorities and Governments is an excellent and appropriate intent. We hope that the Working Group will take that intent one step further and hear the prayer of the African-American representatives. Expert dialogue with the US Government on the subject of African-American reparations would, at this time, be one of the few ways in which the Working Group could serve to promote mutual understanding between the minority in question and the Government.

There is another role that I believe the Working Group could expand upon, and that is in assisting the African-American minority in its efforts at self-organization. African-Americans have a well documented collective experience which is of the essence to all minorities: that of the complete annihilation of identity and severing of ties to ancestry and the consequences of this criminal act upon the collective human spirit. The Working Group could invite African-Americans to share their accumulated wisdom with other minorities and with the experts, in the form of a written document. An invitation to share experience would have a beneficial effect as follows.

First, African-Americans in the US are to a great degree convinced that the US Government controls the UN. They have been very slow in believing that the United Nations will be able to do anything of substance for them, and it has been difficult for us to argue that the UN will recognize their suffering in a meaningful way. If the Working Group on Minorities were to invite African-Americans to share their experience in the form of a written document, the word would spread within the African-American communities that the UN is listening. Just this act of listening can serve to promote the self-organization of African-Americans.

Additionally, an invitation to prepare an official document of experience would facilitate the gathering together of a core group of Black leaders and intellectuals. In our view, this core group could potentially evolve into the foundation of a council or governing body.

Finally, I would like to make one small comment on the commentary to the Declaration on the Rights of Minorities prepared by Professor Eide. The commentaries are very helpful and very much appreciated. As to the importance of identity in Article 1.1, I would say that we view identity as equal in importance to physical life. The individual human being enjoys physical life: the collective enjoys a collective spirit which is identity. Both the life of the body and the life of the human spirit are essential. Thank you for listening.

6) Written Statement to the 52nd Session of the Sub-Commission

on the Promotion and Protection of Human Rights, August 2000

Agenda Item 8, Prevention of Discrimination Against and Protection of Minorities

The lingering effects of plantation slavery have left my people and me in a deprived state. We are deprived of our original identity. We, the so-called African-Americans, have experienced the forcible removal of culture, religion and 'mother tongue'. The annihilation of our 'mother tongue' is the extermination of our identity.

To the extent that we have been deprived of our culture, our religion and our language, we do not have our human rights. We have been dispossessed of those human rights possessed by every minority and people and protected by the United Nations. While we are a People, and not a minority, in the United States we are placed within a minority status. We mimic the human rights of the majority; but in reality, we are in the position of a minority, as every scholar knows.

The United States of America has destroyed our human rights. It has covered us over with its own, fraudulently, by trick and by duress. We were buried and hidden, so very much so that United Nations in making its laws has left us out, it seems: it is not known immediately where we fit. To be left out of both the Declaration on the Rights of Minorities, and the International Covenant on Civil and Political Rights, is to not have political recognition of our human rights. Thus, we feel we can not intelligently argue the issue of a violation of our human rights. While we are human, we have not been in possession of our human rights for the past 400 years. Our human rights were willfully destroyed, utterly. They were destroyed by the slave masters, under the auspices of the United States central and local governments, during our long sojourn as slaves in America.

We, the so-called African-Americans, were taken away from the culture of our origin. The slave ship took us away from our ancestral religious belief. Regarding our original language, there were not any provisions set in motion by the local and federal governments of America for us to cultivate and continue speaking our language. To the contrary, originally, provisions were set in motion to prevent us from speaking our language. We were intentionally separated from one another with total disregard, during slavery, such that we would not be able to speak our language. Ultimately, we lost the knowledge of it.

By forcibly stripping us of the use of our language and of the right to be educated in the same, the Government of the United States deracinated our collective identity, making our condition irreversible. Absent exposure to our original tongue at the earliest possible stages in life and in primary and secondary levels of schooling, how could and can we speak it with other members of our community and preserve our individual identity? The United States causes us to remain trapped within the Anglo-American culture regenerating its 'mother tongue', in reality, its identity.

When we are able to argue about a violation of our human rights, this is our complaint: we are human beings, but to this date and time we are denied the human right of speaking our 'mother tongue' in violation of Article 27 of the International

Covenant on Civil and Political Rights, which the United States of America has ratified.

The United States grants the right today for us to speak our language. Then speak it, one might say. How can we speak what the U.S. has denied us the use of? If our 'mother tongue' is taken away, aren't we denied the use of it? No! One may say, you are deprived of the use of it; there is a difference. Is not to be deprived of the use of our 'mother tongue' the same as being denied the use of it? No! Says the State, to be denied the use of it presupposes it is in your possession; while being deprived of its use presupposes it has been taken away. Well, since it has been taken away, we are both deprived and denied the use of it. The very act of taking our 'mother tongue' away was for the express purpose of denying us the use of it. In fact, the act is tantamount to a permanent ongoing denial.

Thus, this will be viewed as a gross and an excessive act of denial of the U.S. to permit the so-called African-Americas to speak their 'mother tongue' in community with other members of their group. While the act of the U.S. may be viewed as a violation of the Convention on the Non-Applicability of Statutory Limitations to War Crimes and Crimes Against Humanity, which the U.S. has not signed or ratified, the U.S. has made itself responsible for the rights of minorities, within its jurisdiction, to not be denied the use of their own language in community with other members of their group. We cannot speak ours. The U.S. grossly denies us the right, having deprived us, continually, of the very instrument. And in its place, the U.S. continually has forced its Anglo-Saxon 'mother tongue' upon us for the past 400 years. Absent our 'mother tongue', we are a non-people, living without a permanent identity.

We have brought our prayers to the Working Group on Minorities, as it has been entrusted with the task of promoting the rights of minorities. We wish to thank the Working Group on Minorities. We appreciate and applaud their efforts and join with them in the recommendation that a Regional Seminar for the Americas be held in order to examine the issues of African-Americans in the Americas.

In conclusion, we, so-called African-Americans, support the notion that "Race" is a constituent element of the definition of a minority. In the U.S. Blacks are mindful, daily, of a consciousness of "otherness", with respect to racial differences, as every scholar knows. And, unlike the Indigenous Peoples who were native to the territory, before colonization, and who formed many groups and spoke several languages, African-Americans were displaced from their common territory, and yet they invoke their similar characteristics in order to obtain their rights. As the so-called African-American "Racial" group is a group destroyed, it is axiomatic knowledge that we are a different racial group from the majority: we have neither racial dignity nor political bond.

The integration movement of the 1960s, whatever of high hope and of good intention, it did not make us equal with the majority, nor did it set us apart as a people or as a minority. We continued to mimic the human rights of the majority. At the same hour, during the 1960s, there had long been developing in the U.S. not only a consciousness of "otherness", but also an awareness to bring that consciousness into reality. The Ethno-racial differences had then reached the glass ceiling, marked by violent rioting in major cities: Watts, California; Newark, New Jersey; Rochester, New York; Cleveland, Ohio; Cincinnati, Ohio; Chicago, Illinois; Harlem, New York; Detroit, Michigan; Washington D.C.; and Atlanta, Georgia in the time period from 1965 through 1967.

U.S. federal agents cleared the way for a non-violent solution. The US Government and its media sought to redirect the rising Black consciousness, by promoting integration. Non-violent integration's chief advocate was the late and the memorable Dr. Martin Luther King Jr., who fell to his unfortunate death from an assassin's bullet in the year 1968, having commenced the civil rights movement December 1, 1955.

7) Oral Statement to the 52nd Session of the Sub-Commission

on the Promotion and Protection of Human Rights, August 2000

Agenda Item 8, Minorities

We appreciate and applaud the efforts of the Working Group on Minorities and we join with them in the recommendation that a Regional Seminar for the Americas be held in order to examine the issues of African-Americans, in the Americas. Thirty-one African-American organizations from the grassroots to the intellectual elite stand with us today in support of the proposed Regional Seminar for the Americas.

I came to the Sub-Commission to seek recognition that we, the so-called African-Americans, do not fit the UN established definition of human beings, in the category of minority or as a People. The United States has the UN under the belief that we do fit, one or the other, in that the US asserts that the UN is in charge of promoting and protecting the inherent rights of human beings - everyone, everywhere. To the extent that we do not fit the UN definition, presently, the UN definition is in need of expansion to also include us. For we have not our original 'mother tongue', culture nor religion, thus, no identity: due to the lingering effects of plantation slavery. We are but clones of the Anglo-Saxon in the United States. During slavery, we were forced to speak the Anglo-Saxon's mother tongue, and practice their religion and culture. Our human rights were destroyed.

Therefore, like the Indigenous People, it is our preference to be reinstated as a "people," in that we have been historically categorized by continental ancestry, from which territory we were shackled and removed. We invoked that characteristic in order to obtain our rights. Notwithstanding, we have brought our prayer to the Working Group on Minorities, as it has been entrusted with the task of promoting and protecting rights of minorities, in which category we are placed in the US. We support the notion that "Race" is a constituent element of the definition of a minority. My people are the living evidence of a group with a consciousness of " otherness," of difference, having been victims of four hundred years of plantation slavery, by the rigor of "Racial" grouping.

Written and Oral Statements to the UN in 1999

Statements delivered in 1999 were heard and responded to by the UN. Statements were delivered by Mr. Silis Muhammad unless otherwise noted.

1. Written Statement to the Commission on Human Rights, April 1999

2. Oral Statement to the Commission on Human Rights

3. Oral Statement to the Working Group on Minorities, May 1999

4. Oral Statement of Attorney Harriett AbuBakr to the Working Group on Minorities

5. Oral Statement of Ida Hakim to the Working Group on Minorities

6. Written Statement to the Sub-Commission on the Promotion and Protection of Human Rights, August 1999

7. Oral Statement to the Sub-Commission on the Promotion and Protection of Human Rights

1) Written Statement to the 55th session of the Commission on Human Rights

Agenda item 14. Specific groups and individuals: (b) Minorities:

I am Silis Muhammad, spiritual son of the Honorable Elijah Muhammad. But for him, we so-called African-Americans would not have the courage to make the following statement to the Commission on Human Rights. Of this I am sure. We thank him for the great good he did for us, and perchance too for humanity.

Our question is whether we, the so-called African-Americans in the United States of America, are in possession of our human rights.

Article 27 of the International Covenant on Civil and Political Rights, which the United States of America has ratified, states, "In those States in which ethnic, religious or linguistic minorities exist, persons belonging to such minorities shall not be denied the right, in community with other members of their group, to enjoy their own culture, to profess and practice their own religion, or to use their own language."

We, the so-called African-Americans, were taken away from the culture of our origin. The slave ship took us from our place of beginning, as you well do know. The slave master did not return us to our culture, nor did he bring our culture and teach it to us. Nor has the Government of the United States of America, to date, sought to teach us our culture, or return us to it. We are absent the knowledge of our cultural beginning.

The slave ship took us away from our ancestral religious belief. We were dislodged from the knowledge of our lineage to Allah, God. The slave master taught us of his religion ultimately, and of his lineage to a supreme being whom he refers to by the name of God. The federal or local governments of America did not teach nor make provisions for us, the so-called African-Americans, or slaves, to learn the knowledge of our transmissible religious belief. We are absent the knowledge of our ancestral tradition of religion.

Regarding our original language, there were not any provisions set in motion by the local and federal governments of America for us to cultivate and continue speaking our language. To the contrary, provisions were set in motion to prevent us from speaking our language, originally. We were intentionally separated from one another, with total disregard, during slavery such that we would not be able to speak our language. Ultimately, we lost the knowledge of it.

Thus, to the extent that we were deprived of our culture, our religion and our language, we are not in possession of our human rights. Moreover, to the extent that we, especially during the period of chattel slavery, were constrained by the laws, the culture, the religion and the language of the Anglo-American, we lived, and to this day live, under a tyrannical government. By the acts of forced assimilation the Anglo-Americans have sought also to subsume us, the African-Americans, into its Constitution.

The desires, the perpetual existence and the human rights of African-Americans are not embodied in the majority Constitution, which, from its origin, is absent any input from us. The laws arising from America's majority Constitution do not embody the living will of the African-Americans.

Thus, we feel we cannot intelligently argue the issue of violation of our human rights. While we are human, we have not been in possession of our human rights for the past 433 years. Our human rights were willfully destroyed, utterly. They were destroyed by the slave masters, under the auspices of the United States central and local governments, during our long sojourn as slaves in America.

The Universal Declaration of Human Rights states that recognition of the inalienable rights of all members of the human family is the foundation of freedom, justice and peace in the world. Here, at the beginning of the histories of the so-called African-Americans, the enslaved Africans brought to America were defined in the same terms as the "cattle" belonging to the Anglo-American rulers. Thus, our rights were those of their "cattle"; ours were not human rights. Yet we were then--and are, still, members of the human family.

Our inalienable rights were distorted so completely, that we are damaged goods, still. We are lost from our original inherent culture, religion and language. America cannot lawfully force us to accept the choices which she deems to be our inalienable rights; nor can she force us and our progeny to abandon the hope for the reclamation of our own. One hundred thirty four years of forced assimilation has not abrogated the desire to know, and to be ourselves. Today, we have no permanent national recognition, as a result of slavery. We have been identified as slaves, Niggers, Negroes, Coloreds, Black-Americans and today we are so-called African-Americans.

Thus, we are to this day a revolving nation, suspended within a nation: rent from our roots, as a result of slavery and its lingering effects. We are detached, still, from our inalienable rights. To this extent, the very foundation upon which freedom, justice and peace among nations is established is for us non-existing: our inalienable rights are extinct! Recognition of inalienable rights, for us, is a faith hoped for. And this poses a threat to peace for the United States of America, for the Americas and potentially for Europe. Why? It is a threat because of the despair of the many: which will endlessly be ignited to loathing and, or rioting. It will be ignited, lawlessly, by the perpetual humanitarian desires of the few: if the fever, or this abnormal situation, is not reversed by the few humanitarians who aim lawfully and by sanctions to efficaciously stamp out violations of the Universal Declaration of Human Rights. As in the contemporary case of Iraq, the U.N., urged by the United States, sent inspectors to Iraq so as to avert what America believes to be a threat to humanity.

The United States of America, for the past fifty years, has violated this august Universal Declaration of Human Rights. During the past fifty years, America has not seen fit to restore us to our inalienable rights, or them to us; nor has she seen fit to grant to us the choice to be, or not to be Americans. Therefore, this statement is a request for United Nations assistance in the establishment of a forum (perhaps under the auspices of the Sub-Commission.) The type of forum requested is similar to the one opened for the Aboriginal peoples in Geneva. We wish that the United Nations will establish a forum within the boundaries of the United States, preferably at United Nations Headquarters.

The Government of the United States ordained slavery and forced assimilation upon captive Africans for more than four hundred years. The United States Government wishes to persuade the United Nations and the world, today, that African-Americans are full and equal members of America's society, enjoying inalienable rights. Their propaganda is so persuasive and effective that even some of us believe that the self determination of the Anglo-American is our very own.

The Universal Declaration of Human Rights states, "disregard and contempt for human rights have resulted in barbarous acts which have outraged the conscience of mankind...." America's disregard and contempt for human rights ought to be seen by the United Nations as she has dispossessed us of our culture, religion and language and has forced assimilation upon us. Indeed it is barbarous, and it denies us the full enjoyment of freedom, justice and equality.

"Whereas," according to the Universal Declaration of Human Rights, "it is essential, if man is not to be compelled to have recourse, as a last resort, to rebellion against tyranny and oppression, that human rights should be protected by the rule of law." Here, we seek the persuasive powers as well as the rule of law of the United Nations, and its member states to come to our aid.

African-Americans have looked toward and exhausted all remedies made available by the majority government, although, it is viewed as the oppressor. In light of the aforementioned, cannot the United Nations open a forum for African-Americans in its host country? We wish to address the question of whether we choose to reclaim or recapture our original culture, language, religion and identity, or whether we choose to assimilate into the majority culture of America. Upon this matter we have never enjoyed the freedom of choice. We pray to the Commission on Human Rights for the right to make our choice within the protection of a United Nations forum.

We want recognition of our choice of human rights. We want recognition of our choice of inalienable rights. We want the crime of plantation slavery, and its lingering effects which was, and is still, a crime against us and against humanity, to be rectified. We believe that through a forum we can assist the United Nations in fulfilling its most noble covenant, the Universal Declaration of Human Rights, which envisages human rights "for everyone, everywhere;" as at present, we are left out!

2) Oral Statement to the 55th Session of the Commission on Human Rights, April 1999

Agenda Item 14(b) Specific Groups and Individuals: Minorities

Madam Chairperson:

Our question is whether the United States of America's refusal to ratify certain U.N. human rights treaties, which would lead to the restoration of the human rights of her handicapped victims of slavery, amounts to a violation of the Universal Declaration of Human Rights.

The Universal Declaration of Human Rights envisages the establishment of a common framework of protected human rights for everyone, everywhere. The United States knew, upon the adoption of the Universal Declaration on December 10, 1948, that African-Americans did not have their original mother's tongue, their inherent religion or their ancestral culture, as a result of the acts of the Anglo-American government. She had kept us perpetually regenerating the human rights of the Anglo-American, against our will.

Our identity as a national minority, a minority or as a people, in possession of our human rights, can not ever be achieved if left to the will of the United States. Why? America's refusal to ratify the Convention on the Non-applicability of Statutory Limitations to War Crimes and Crimes Against Humanity makes it blatantly clear that she shuns responsibility for 400 years of slavery and its legacies. In the process she obstructs the pathway for the restoration of our human rights.

The United States holds herself out as being in full compliance with the spirit of U.N. protected human rights for everyone, everywhere; while holding us in this slavery predicament. Thereby she causes the U.N. to fail in its intent to consider everyone, everywhere; and causes us to remain trapped within the identity of the Anglo-American.

Her omission to act, with knowledge that there was an equitable and fiduciary duty to act, is not within the spirit of the Universal Declaration. We will remain victims continuously, until the United Nations corrects the damages that the U.S. has done to it and to us. Thus the United States has committed fraud against the U.N., ongoing forced assimilation against us, and an additional act calculated to bring about our total destruction.

Thus we conclude, that since its inception, a ***consistent violation of the Universal Declaration of Human Rights*** has been perpetrated by the United States. We ask, humbly, can this lofty body, the Commission on Human Rights, permit the U.S. to continue these acts?

We ask the U.N. to grant us a forum for the purpose of restoring our human rights, our political being, and our status as a people. Within a forum, while promoting respect for the Universal Declaration, we will be able to rebuild a kind of council or governing body amongst ourselves, absent the social engineering of the U.S. Government. We will develop and present a package of recommendations to benefit race relations in American society, including support for those of us who wish to migrate to a friendly nation.

In closing, 50 years after the signing of the Universal Declaration of Human Rights, my people stand before you seeking political resurrection and restoration of our human rights.

3) Oral Statement to the Working Group on Minorities, May 1999

Agenda Item 3. b), 8 (a) Examination of the causes and nature of the problems affecting minorities and group accommodation, and their possible solutions, including: - the legacies of the slave trade on the black communities throughout the Americas; - issues relating to the forcible displacement of populations.

Greetings Mr. Chairman, Members of the Working Group on Minorities.

The lingering effects of plantation slavery have left me and my people in a state of genocide. Genocide is to a group as homicide is to an individual. Rent from our land, our roots, sold and forced into slavery: we have been recognized as slaves, Niggers, Negroes, Coloreds, Black-Americans and today we are the so-called African-Americans. We are more than 40 million, and yet we are a people dead. We have been dead, as slaves, for 400 years. Is not our struggle for human dignity equally as important as groups fighting for their human life. To be alive, with the knowledge that I am, as a man, dead, is worse than physical death. Death of the physical body sets you free. Death of the human spirit is a living hell.

Commencing with slavery to this date, we are a revolving nation, within the nation of America. We are absent our foundation-- our human rights: culture, religion and mother's tongue. We have lost our original identity.

Our question is whether America's refusal to ratify a particular U.N. human rights treaty, which would lead to the restoration of our identity, amounts to a violation of the Universal Declaration of Human Rights. The Declaration on the Rights of Persons Belonging to National or Ethnic, Religious and Linguistic Minorities flows from the Universal Declaration of Human rights. The Universal Declaration envisages, to quote Professor Eide, "the establishment of a common framework of protected human rights for everyone, everywhere."

The United States knew, upon the adoption of the Universal Declaration on December 10, 1948, that African-Americans did not have their original mother's tongue, their inherent religion or their ancestral culture. America did not have us in mind at the time of signing that document; or she had the intent to persuade the U.N. that she did. To the extent that the United Nations left us out of the Universal Declaration of Human Rights, the government of the United States has designed a falsehood which has hampered the United Nations and its member states. We have been left out of the Declaration on the Rights of Minorities also, because of this falsehood.

Our identity as a people, in possession of our human rights, can not ever be achieved if left to the will of the United States. Why? America's refusal to ratify the Convention on the Non-applicability of Statutory Limitations to War Crimes and Crimes Against Humanity, in 1968, some twenty (20) years after the adoption of the Universal Declaration, makes it blatantly clear, again, that she did not have in mind human rights for everyone, everywhere.

The United States' omission to ratify that particular convention reveals the intent of the U.S. Government at the moment and time of her act. Her thinking is consistent with her thinking in 1948. Either she did not have us in mind; or she seeks specifically to block the pathway to our human rights. While holding us in this ever revolving state, the United States holds herself out as being in full compliance with the spirit of U.N. protected human rights for everyone, everywhere; and causes us to remain trapped within the Anglo-American culture, regenerating her religion and tongue, in reality, her identity.

The United States has committed fraud against the U.N., genocide against us. Thus we conclude, that since its inception, a ***consistent violation of the Universal Declaration of Human Rights*** has been perpetrated by the United States.

We ask you to recommend to the Sub-Commission the establishment of a forum, with expert guidance, for the purpose of restoring our human rights -- which only we can reclaim or choose: our legal, political being and status as a people. Within a forum, we will 1) promote respect for the Universal Declaration of human rights amongst ourselves, which will ultimately include the Diaspora; we will 2) rebuild a kind of council or governing body amongst ourselves, absent the social engineering of the U.S. Government. Within this council we will 3) openly discuss the devolution, in pertinent parts, of the Constitution of the United States, which defines us as three-fifths of a human being. This package will be presented to the United States. The venture commenced, intelligence can be gained for the Sub-Commission that might usefully 4) address the continuing legal, political and economic legacies of the slave trade as experienced by the victims. We will 5) discuss reclamation, restoration, repatriation, reparations and migration of some of us to a friendly nation. We want these discussions to 6) benefit race relations in the society of the United States. The establishment of a forum for the reasons stated, would also eliminate the burden of slavery for America's future generation.

In closing, we thank the Working Group for including in its agenda the legacies of the slave trade.

4) Statement to the Working Group on Minorities by Attorney Harriett AbuBakr

Provisional Agenda Item 3. b), 8 (a) Examination of the causes and nature of the problems affecting minorities and group accommodation, and their possible solutions, including: - the legacies of the slave trade on the black communities throughout the Americas;

- issues relating to the forcible displacement of populations

Greetings Mr. Chairman, and greetings to the esteemed members of the Working Group on Minorities. I would like to thank you for placing the legacies of the slave trade on the black communities throughout the Americas on your agenda. I believe it is appropriate that a study of our condition begins here, and I trust the experts in this Working Group to consider our experiences, past and present, in light of the law.

My name is Harriett AbuBakr. I am a founding member of the National Commission for Reparations, and an attorney at law. Victims come to me in my practice, relying upon my knowledge and my reputation as a defender of their rights. Therefore it is not in the manner of an organization leader that I come to you. I come to you as a victim, relying upon your knowledge of law and your reputation as defenders of my rights. We African Americans are thankful for your recognition of us and for the recognition that the Sub-Commission gave to us in its resolution 1998/24. As a people, we have waited so long for experts to study and understand what has been done to us. I urge you to continue to invest your considerable moral strength and legal expertise in analyzing our unique situation.

While you listen to my intervention, please consider how you would define the crime that was and is being committed against us, how you would protect our rights, and what means you see for our restoration.

African-Americans in the United States of America are not the same people as the Africans who were kidnaped and sold into slavery during the European slave trade. Those Africans no longer exist racially, physically, culturally, mentally or spiritually. They were intentionally destroyed, and their descendants are a different people; changed in ways that are permanent, and damaged in ways that are making recovery difficult.

Medical studies indicate that because of the extreme physical torment and illness we suffered while being shipped to the Americas, only those Africans whose bodies retained fluids and salts were able to survive. This torment caused a genetic change in our population which manifests today as a far greater than average incidence of high blood pressure and the resulting heart attacks and strokes. African Americans today still die from the torment of the middle passage. We cannot reverse genetic changes.

Throughout the 310 years of slavery, African women were raped by their owners and forced to bear children of mixed race. This brought about the second change in our population. Through force, against the will of African women, and with intent to destroy us as a race, this crime was committed. Today the vast majority of African Americans have Caucasians among their ancestors. We cannot reverse the mixing of the slave master's blood into ours, although many of us would remove it if we could.

During slavery certain black males were singled out like stud horses and used in order to populate a plantation with bigger, stronger slaves. Through forced breeding, our physique is not the same as our African ancestors. In part because of breeding, and the food that we were forced to eat, we are today a people with extraordinary health problems. We suffer from a far greater than average incidence of diabetes, prostate cancer and obesity. We cannot reverse the changes in our physical condition - we can only strive to live with them.

In addition to being changed genetically, racially and physically, many millions of us have died. The United Nations has been exceedingly concerned about the loss of six million Jews in a crime which is commonly referred to as the greatest example of genocide. And yet we have lost many more than six million. The lowest estimate of our loss is 10 million, and the highest up to 500 million. Our people were thrown overboard ships, beaten to death, hung, starved, torn apart and burned to death. We can hardly name the many different ways in which we have died.

Even today a mass grave of 400 African Americans slaughtered in a race riot, is being uncovered. And the killing hasn't ended. You see us marching in protest because our young men and women are being killed by police at an alarming rate. Amnesty International has reported to the U.N. on this. Amnesty International has also just reported that the United States is administering the death penalty on a disproportionate number of Black men. How many millions of us have to die before we are recognized as victims of something more criminal than racial discrimination?

In addition to being forcibly changed and murdered, we have been destroyed culturally. The cultural life of the original African slaves was completely obliterated in the United States. As individuals, African Americans have no idea of what country, what region of Africa, what tribe, or what culture they came from. When we realize that not only can we not speak our mother's tongue, but we can never know who our ancestral Mothers were, we suffer an immeasurable grief. How degrading - how sad - how lonely to have lost all trace of our Mothers and Fathers, never to be able to find them again, even within ourselves. As a people we are just beginning to wake up to the knowledge of our loss, and to feel this grief. As a people, everything that we were is dead.
It is perhaps for this reason that we have come to the United Nations. We want to live again as ourselves, anew, and we need help.

Mentally, we have been changed also. Our African ancestors were subjected to trans-generational traumatic stress. They suffered terrorism from the time of their birth until their death, living their entire lives with an unnatural fear of white people. Up unto and including this very generation, an unreasonable fear of white people can be discovered in some of the strongest of Black men. Black youth, in overcoming fear, have substituted a "kamikaze" type of anger which waits only to be ignited. Some of them want to be martyrs. We believe it is only our effort at a legal solution that holds them in check. In addition to fear and anger, a mental condition of self hatred came into existence as a result of slavery. This condition affects us today, causing us to turn on ourselves and each other, effectively preventing our recovery.

Perhaps the most destructive thing that was done to us was that a white Christian God was placed over us, a captive people. The Christian religion was used to subjugate us as slaves, and it continues to subjugate us today. It is pressed upon our sons and daughters by their own well meaning mothers and fathers, with little knowledge that a white God may not be the best God for a Black child.

In closing, I would like to ask again how you would define the crime that was and is being committed against us, how you would protect our rights, and what means you see for our restoration. I am convinced that there are ways in which you can help us almost immediately, and I urge you to help us immediately, as many of us are descending into an apathetic condition.

I urge you to act on our behalf. I urge you to recommend to the Sub-Commission that a forum for African Americans be established at the U.N. in New York, as was requested last year by Mr. Silis Muhammad. I urge you to recommend to the Sub-Commission that a new Working Group be established here in Geneva to study our condition throughout the Diaspora. I urge you to recommend that the Sub-Commission pass a resolution recognizing slavery and the slave trade as a crime against humanity. I urge you to take up the task of writing a working paper as a way to begin analyzing our situation. I urge you to visit the United States and visit us, in order that we might demonstrate to you our condition. And finally, I urge you to include us in the Declaration on the Rights of Persons Belonging to National or Ethnic, Religious and Linguistic Minorities, or if that cannot be done, I urge you to begin writing a new declaration for us.

Thank you for your kind attention.

5) Statement to the Working Group on Minorities by Ida Hakim

Provisional Agenda Item 3. b), 8 (a) Examination of the causes and nature of the problems affecting minorities and group accommodation, and their possible solutions, including: - the legacies of the slave trade on the black communities throughout the Americas;

- **issues relating to the forcible displacement of populations**

Greetings Mr. Chairman and members of the Working Group on Minorities. I am pleased to be able to intervene under the agenda item 3. b). With your agenda you have given voice to African Americans from the United States and throughout the Diaspora. In so doing you give courage to us and you renew our hope for a peaceful solution to a situation which has the potential to become an unprecedented race war.

First I would like to comment on the legacies of the slave trade. In the United States of America, the crime wasn't only trans-generational chattel slavery, and it isn't only genocide against a people, it is a crime against all of humanity. To leave it uncorrected is a crime against even me.

The European slave trade was a hideously immoral undertaking in which the church, governments, businesses and individuals participated. Such a wrong, left uncorrected, give us, the inheritors of the wrong, a desolate legacy. I offer as evidence the United States of America: the place where many white people feel they just naturally deserve the privileges, and they are willing to take their own kind of special measures to make sure Africans Americans, as a people, don't get the upper hand. America is the place where more moral outrage can be shown at the killing of a dog than at the killing of a homeless Blackman. America is the place where white privileged children murder other children because they are bored, they don't feel good, and they want attention. We are in a morally desolate condition. We need an opportunity for a new legacy. We need a redemptive opportunity.

You are experts on human rights, and therefore you have moral authority. Through your help, the people of the United States may be persuaded to see the value of correcting wrongs, doing away with white privilege, and establishing true freedom, justice and equality. Your Declaration on the Rights of Persons Belonging to National or Ethnic, Religious and Linguistic Minorities offers guidance which can be used to bring justice to situations involving minorities. We wish that it had made mention of how to first restore to African Americans their rights and then protect them. I speak of a people who have been forcibly displaced and, in the United States, subsumed by a government whose intention toward them has never been to offer them human rights. Perhaps you would consider making revisions to the Declaration if at all possible.

The Working Group on Minorities is able to make recommendations to the Sub-Commission. These recommendations can potentially start the "wheels" of the UN turning with respect to the legacies of the slave trade. The members of the Working Group can help African Americans find their way into having meaningful protection of the law. We read and study what you, the experts, write. We ask that you consider some possible steps that we recommend, and respond to us with your opinion.

Consider the great understanding that could come from a UN sponsored forum for African Americans, as described by Mr. Silis Muhammad in his intervention. Consider the constructive changes that could take place if the Working Group on Minorities would engage a team of experts to report on the legacies of the slave trade. Consider the progress that could be made in changing the moral condition in the U.S. if human rights educators were to teach that the slave trade destroyed more of humanity and created more contemporary victims than Nazi crimes and apartheid. Consider the confidence that you would build if you place a direct response to African Americans in your report to the Sub-Commission. So much good can come from facing up to the truth and facing up to a hard task.

We would also like to ask for the help of some of the United Nations Specialized Agencies.

From the World Health Organization we would like to see a study of the health legacies of the slave trade. African Americans suffer from a number of medical problems including high blood pressure, heart attack, stroke, diabetes and prostate cancer. These diseases are found in the African American people to a greater degree than the rest of the Americcan population. Medical studies indicate that permanent physical changes may have occurred during slavery. We believe the World Health Organization could help bring together the facts behind this issue.

We ask the International Labor Organization to look into America's privately owned prisons. America's prisons are filled with African American men who are engaged in making products for private corporations. Many earn only a few pennies an hour. It is certainly reminiscent of the slave trade, to watch American big business reap profit from a racially discriminatory judicial system and a constitution which permits slavery when a person has been convicted of a crime. We are confident that the ILO is aware of this situation. Perhaps there have been labor union objections to the "slavery like" use of prisoners in the United States. We ask the ILO to look into this situation if at all possible.

From UNESCO we would like to see a study of what happens to a people when they are torn away from everything they know and forced to stop speaking their language, singing their songs, remembering their home and praying to their God. What do they go through over generations? How far from their nature can they be driven? What possible assistance can be offered to help them return. We ask if UNESCO could begin to focus on this. We also ask these organizations to give us their suggestions as to how they believe they might help in finding solutions.

Thank you again, Mr. Chairman and the members of the Working Group on Minorities for placing on your agenda the legacies of the slave trade. My hope is that next year African Americans may be able to intervene in response to progress stemming from actions that you have taken on their behalf. Mr. Silis Muhammad expressed to me his deep appreciation for the Working Group. You are personally thanked for your sympathetic concern, your assistance, and your careful guidance.

6) Written Statement to the 51st session of the Sub-Commission on Prevention of Discrimination and Protection of Minorities, August 1999

Provisional Agenda Item 8, Prevention of discrimination against and the protection of minorities

The lingering effects of plantation slavery have left me and my people in a state of genocide. Genocide is to a group as homicide is to an individual. Rent from our land, our roots, sold and forced into slavery: we have been recognized as slaves, Niggers, Negroes, Coloreds, Black-Americans and today we are the so-called African-Americans. We are more than 40 million, and yet we are a people dead. We have been dead, as slaves, for 400 years. Is not our struggle for human dignity equally as important as that of groups at war for their human life? Ours is a war of the mind. The U.N. will send troops to protect physical life. Is not our war as great? Is not the mind as precious as the body? To be alive, with the knowledge that I am, as a man, dead, is worse than physical death. Death of the physical body sets you free. Death of the human spirit is a living hell.

Beginning with slavery to this date, we are a revolving nation, within the nation of America. We are absent our foundation -- our human rights: culture, religion and mother's tongue. We have lost our original identity. While we are a people, and not a minority, we are treated as a minority by the U.S. Government. Therefore we bring our case to you, the Sub-

Commission on Prevention of Discrimination and the Protection of Minorities.

The Declaration on the Rights of Persons Belonging to National or Ethnic, Religious and Linguistic Minorities, which flows from the Universal Declaration of Human rights, addresses the question of identity. Concomitantly, the Universal Declaration envisages, to quote Professor Eide, "the establishment of a common framework of protected human rights for everyone, everywhere."

The United States knew, upon the adoption of the Universal Declaration on December 10, 1948, that African-Americans did not have their original mother's tongue, their inherent religion or their ancestral culture -- their human identity. America did not have us in mind at the time of signing that document; or she had the intent to persuade the U.N. that she did. To the extent that the United Nations left us out of the Universal Declaration of Human Rights, the government of the United States has designed a falsehood which has hampered the United Nations and its Member States. We have been left out of the Declaration on the Rights of Minorities also, because of this falsehood.

To be left out of both the Declaration on the Rights of Minorities, and the Universal Declaration, is to not have recognition of our human life, politically. We have no identity because we were intentionally deprived of education in our mother's tongue, thus we do not have our own culture. Absent our culture, we exist in a state of civil death.

We are concerned about our right to education in our mother's tongue as we know that it would guarantee us an identity. We appreciate the Declaration on the Rights of Minorities in its focus on education, but we conclude that even if the United States wanted to, she could not restore us to our family roots and our mother's tongue. She cannot trace our lineage except to the continent of Africa, where there exist over 1200 families of languages. Therefore we must be allowed to choose the mother's tongue or tongues that we, as a people, wish to speak. We feel we must have the protection of a U.N. forum as we engage in this stage of the mental war for our identity, lest we be targeted and considered subversive by the U.S. Government.

Our identity as a people, in possession of our human rights, can not ever be achieved if left entirely to the will of the United States. Why? America's refusal to ratify the Convention on the Non-applicability of Statutory Limitations to War Crimes and Crimes Against Humanity, in 1968, some twenty (20) years after the adoption of the Universal Declaration, makes it blatantly clear, again, that she did not have in mind human rights for everyone, everywhere.

The failure of the United States to ratify that particular convention reveals the intent of the U.S. Government at the moment and time of her act. Her thinking is consistent with her thinking in 1948. Either she did not have us in mind; or she seeks specifically to block the pathway to our human rights -- our identity. While holding us in this ever revolving state, the United States holds herself out as being in full compliance with the spirit of U.N. protected human rights for everyone, everywhere; and causes us to remain trapped within the Anglo-American culture, regenerating her religion and tongue, in reality, her identity.

Thus, the United States has committed fraud against the U.N., genocide against us, and we linger in a state of civil death, as our identity has not been preserved. We conclude, that since its inception, a ***consistent violation of the Universal***

Declaration of Human Rights has been perpetrated by the United States.

We recommend the establishment of a U.N. forum, with expert guidance, for African Americans in the U.S. We want the forum to be located at U.N. Headquarters in New York. We believe that the United Nations has an equitable and moral obligation to persuade the United States to financially provide for the forum inasmuch as the fraudulent acts of the U.S. Government have hampered the U.N. in fulfilling its obligation of protected human rights for everyone, everywhere. Surely there ought to be grave concern that more than 40 million people have been left out, and do not have their protected human rights. If the U.S. Government refuses to financially support a forum, we would gratefully accept the sponsorship of the United Nations or any sympathetic government.

We want a forum for the purpose of restoring our human rights -- which only we can reclaim or choose: our legal, political being and status as a people. Within a forum, we will 1) promote respect for the Universal Declaration of human rights amongst ourselves, which will ultimately include the Diaspora; we will 2) rebuild a kind of council or governing body amongst ourselves, absent the social engineering of the U.S. Government. Within this council we will 3) openly discuss the devolution, in pertinent parts, of the Constitution of the United States, which defines us as three-fifths of a human being; we will 4) make choices on the mother's tongue or tongues that we, as a people, wish to speak; we will 5) discuss reclamation, restoration, repatriation, reparations and migration of some of us to a friendly nation.

This package will be presented to the United States. The venture commenced, intelligence can be gained for the Sub-

Commission that might usefully address the continuing legal, political and economic legacies of the slave trade as experienced by the victims. We want these discussions to benefit race relations in the society of the United States. The establishment of a forum for the reasons stated, would also eliminate the burden of slavery for America's future generation.

7) Oral Statement to the Sub-Commission on Prevention of Discrimination

and the Protection of Minorities, August, 1999

Provisional Agenda Item 8: Prevention of discrimination against and the protection of minorities

While we, the so-called African Americans, are a people and not a minority, in the United States we are placed within a minority status. Hence, we call upon the U.N. to come to our succor both under Article 27 of the International Covenant on Civil and Political Rights: the one the U.S. has ratified; and under the Declaration on the Rights of Persons Belonging to National or Ethnic, Religious and Linguistic Minorities, adopted by the United Nations General Assembly in resolution 47/135 of 18 December, 1992.

We charge **civil death.** The U.S., with knowledge that it has denied us our identity for the past 400 years, is in violation of both the aforementioned Covenant and Declaration. In articles 2 and 4, the Declaration stipulates that minorities have the right to protect their culture and identity.

Professor Guillaume Siemienski's working paper on Education rights of minorities: Hague Recommendation states that language, but not just any language, one's "mother tongue" is intimately bound with identity.

Professor Mustapha Mehedi defines the essence of identity in his writings on education. He states, the discovery of one's own identity means not that it is mapped out in isolation, but that it is negotiated (infused) through a dialogue, partly external, partly internal, with others. Education plays a fundamental role in the formation of personal identity. Thus, the right to education is an identity right.

Owing to plantation slavery, intercultural education is an impossibility for us. By forcibly depriving us of our "mother tongue," the Government of the U.S. deracinated our collective identity, making our condition irreversible. We need specific U.N. assistance.

Absent knowledge of our mother tongue, how could and can we speak it with other members of our community, and preserve our individual identity? The annihilation of our "mother tongue" is the extermination of our identity. Absent our identity, we do not have our own culture. Absent culture, we are in a state of civil death. To destroy a people and their shared life is a crime.

The U.N. can provide a remedy by establishing a forum for so-called African-Americans at the U.N. in New York. We want a forum for the purpose of restoring our human rights -- which only we can reclaim or choose. Within a forum, we will 1) rebuild a kind of council or governing body amongst ourselves; 2) openly discuss the devolution, in pertinent parts, of the Constitution of the U.S., which defines us as three-fifth of a human being; 3) make choices on the "mother tongue" or tongues we wish to speak; 4) discuss and conclude on the issues of reclamation, restoration, reparations and migration of some of us to a friendly nation; 5) then present this package to the U.N. in order that the U.N. can facilitate dialogue between us and the U.S. Government.

The forum will provide a peaceful and protected environment for the resurrection of our legal, political being and status as a people. To finance the forum, we would gratefully accept the sponsorship of the U.N. or any compassionate government which aims at **liberty.**

In closing, we thank the Sub-Commission for calling upon the Working Group on Minorities to address the continuing legacies of the slave trade in the Americas and throughout the Diaspora.

Written and Oral Statements to the UN in 1998

Statements delivered in 1998 were heard and responded to by the UN. Oral statements were delivered by Mr. Silis Muhammad unless otherwise noted.

Documents of 1998 in order of presentation:

1) Written Statement to the Commission on Human Rights, April 1998

2) Oral Statement to the Working Group on Minorities, May 1998

3) Oral Statement of Ida Hakim to the Working Group on Minorities

4) Written Statement to the Sub-Commission on the Promotion and Protection of Human Rights, August 1998

5) Oral Statement to the Sub-Commission on the Promotion and Protection of Human Rights

1) Written Statement to the 54th Session of the Commission on Human Rights
Provisional Agenda item 14, Specific Groups and Individuals (b) Minorities
March/April 1998

1. Recognizing that the African National Minority in the U.S.A. has suffered destruction of its ethnic, linguistic, religious and national identity and has been forced to assimilate into the ruling white majority culture: the so-called African Americans make up approximately 12 percent of the U.S. population. They record a 443 year history of slavery, apartheid, and racial discrimination, including 222 years under the authority of the U.S. Government which conferred citizenship upon them without consultation or democratic choice. The U.S. Federal Government officially participated in slavery and in forced cultural assimilation. U.S. State Governments officially participated in slavery, apartheid and racial discrimination. The single attempt to repair the damage of these crimes has been an Affirmative Action program which gave preference not only to African Americans, but to other minorities, women and the disabled. Due to the opposition of white male Americans, and the resulting action of the U.S. Supreme Court, Affirmative Action as a special measure to repair past human rights violations against African Americans, has ceased after 30 years.

2. Knowing that in 1994 a respected African American leader, the Honorable Silis Muhammad, delivered a communication to the U.N. on behalf of African Americans under Communication Procedure 1503: this document offered evidence of human rights crimes, with particular reference to ethnocide and forced assimilation, and it prayed for U.N. assistance, and called for reparations. Regretting that the Working Group on Communications determined that this document failed to show a consistent pattern of gross violations of human rights; and asserting that the enslavement and forced assimilation of African Americans is a part of world history, known to the United Nations, our organization requests that the aforementioned communication, dated March 18, 1994 and entitled Petition for U.N Assistance

Under Resolution 1503 on Behalf of African Americans in the US.A., be examined by the Commission on Human Rights, and its prayer taken into consideration. This communication can be consulted at the Secretariat (see E/CN.4/1997/71 item #C.23).

3. Understanding that the most destructive violation of the human rights of African Americans remains ethnocide and forced assimilation into an alien culture: despite the attempts of American media to portray "happy American blacks" and "wealthy black athletes" the culture of the majority of African Americans is a post slavery culture. Many African Americans have long sought a separate identity, and they have long sought to distinguish themselves from the majority population through unique musical and cultural development. Some African Americans have tried to identify with the African continent and have found that their long absence and forced removal has made them unable to re-connect. African Americans are, in essence, a homeless nation without identity, exploited as a servant class. Increasingly they are being forced into criminal or suspect status.

4. Realizing that African Americans have been represented by a government of their own design for 67 years, with citizenry submitting to their own courts of law and protected by their own military: the Honorable Silis Muhammad, C.E.O. of the Lost-Found Nation of Islam is moving toward independence from the U.S. Government. The Lost-Found Nation of Islam seeks reparations and self-determination. The struggle of African Americans has been a long one, representing over 400 years of resistance and uprisings against repression, torture, duplicity, lynching and murder, political intimidation, harassment and disruption and forced assimilation. That this struggle is finally reaching its culminating stages is evidenced by the submission of the aforementioned petition to the

United Nations under Communication Procedure 1503, and the movement of the Lost-Found Nation of Islam toward independence.

5. In full consideration of the above, we believe that the African American people suffer from gross, systematic and persistent violation of their human rights, particularly their right to self-determination and right to remedy for past and ongoing gross human rights violations. Our organization is concerned with the protection of the human rights of the African National Minority in the U.S.A. We encourage awareness of the potential for racial conflict and violent suppression of those who are seeking independence and reparations. We urge the Commission on Human Rights to assist African Americans in their efforts to recover from official U.S. policies of enslavement, apartheid and forced assimilation.

2) Oral Statement to the Working Group on Minorities, Fourth Session, May 1998
Agenda Item 3 (b) Examining possible solutions to problems involving minorities
including the promotion of mutual understanding between and among minorities and Governments

Greetings to Professor Eide, Members of the Working Group, Representatives of States, NGO's, Scholars, and Guests:

My name is Silis Muhammad. I am a spiritual son of the late Honorable Elijah Muhammad (peace be upon him). Oh, how much he did for us: the so-called African-American, and perchance too for humanity.

Our question is whether the national minority, the so-called African- Americans, are in possession of their inalienable human rights.

Article 27 of the International Covenant on Civil and Political Rights, which the United States of America has ratified, states, "In those States in which ethnic, religious or linguistic minorities exist, persons belonging to such minorities shall not be denied the right, in community with other members of their group, to enjoy their own culture, to profess and practice their own religion, or to use their own language."

Here, the so-called African-Americans are not in possession of their human rights. They were taken away from the culture of their origin. The slave ship took them from their place of beginning, as you scholars well do know. The slave master did not return them to their culture, nor did he bring their culture and teach it to them. Nor has the American government, to date, sought to teach them their culture, or return them to it. They are absent the knowledge of their cultural beginning.

The slave ship took them away from their ancestral religious belief. They were dislodged from the knowledge of their lineage to Allah, God. The slave master taught them of his religion ultimately, and of his lineage to a supreme being whom he refers. to by the name of God. The federal or local governments of America did not teach nor make provisions for the so-called African-American, or slaves, to learn the knowledge of their transmissible religious belief. They are absent the knowledge of their ancestral tradition of religion.

Regarding their original language, there were not any provisions set in motion by the local and federal governments of America for them to cultivate and continue speaking their language. To the contrary, provisions were set in motion to prevent them from speaking their language, originally. They were intentionally separated from one another, with total disregard, during slavery such that they would not be able to speak their language. Ultimately, they lost the knowledge of it.

Thus, to the extent that they were deprived of their culture, their religion and their language, they are not in possession of their human rights. Moreover, to the extent that they, especially during the period of chattel slavery, were constrained by the laws, the culture, the religion and the language of the Anglo-American, they lived, and to this day live, under a tyrannical government. By the acts of forced assimilation the Anglo-American has sought also to subsume the so-called African-American into its Constitution.

The human rights, the desires and the perpetual existence of the national minority are not embodied in the majority Constitution: which, from its origin, is absent any input of the national minority .The laws arising from America's majority Constitution do not embody the living will of the national minority.

Thus, we feel we cannot intelligently argue the issue of (a) violation of our human rights. While we are human, we have not been in possession of (our) human rights for the past 433 years. Our human rights were willfully destroyed, utterly. They were destroyed by the slave masters, under the auspices of the United States central and local governments, during our long sojourn as slaves in America.

The United Nations Universal Declaration of Human Rights states that recognition of the inalienable rights of all members of the human family is the foundation of freedom, justice and peace in the world. Here, at the beginning of the histories of the so-called African-American, the enslaved Africans brought to America were defined in the same terms as the "cattle" belonging to the Anglo-American rulers. Thus, our rights were those of their "cattle"; ours were not human rights.

It is everywhere known, amongst the scholars, that the clause in the Anglo-American Declaration of Independence which states, "all men are created equal, that they are endowed by their Creator with certain unalienable Rights..." did not and does not apply to slaves and to the formerly enslaved.

Embodied in a people's Constitution is the living spirit of their past woes (afflictions), present

wants, beliefs, hopes and the insatiable perpetual will for the control over their own future.

Scholars know well that the essence of the spirit of America's Constitution can be found in the Declaration of Independence. At the time of the formation of America's Constitution and the insertion of the spirit of that clause, so-called African-Americans were slaves. While they were indeed human beings, they were not accorded the respect of being human.

Thus the clause had reference to the Anglo-American sentiments towards the King of England, apparently. The slaves of the Anglo-American, on the eve of the founding of its Constitution, were not members of the same will.

The will of the formerly enslaved so-called African-American, the afflictions, the present wants, beliefs and the aspirations for future hopes were not and are not, today, embodied in spirit in the Constitution of America. The "living will" of the former slave --the present day so-called African-American, cannot be subsumed in the Constitution of America. It is a human right impracticality .It is unrealistic, and therefore a moral wrong: when and wherever it is imposed.

"Inalienable rights" is a power that the majority of African-Americans do not feel, or do not even know they should feel. Their human rights having been demolished, they do not feel the spirit of being protected by the law which arises out of the Constitution. They can merely hope for protection of the law. Justice and peace are powers which only the few hand picked African- Americans can today enjoy, from time to time; but, they too are reminded quite often, that the Anglo-American's power is the only established recognized political power and authority in the United States.

Therefore, this statement is a request for United Nations assistance in the establishment of a forum (perhaps under the auspices of the Sub-Commission), so that the so-called African- Americans' grievances can be expressed, systematically and officially recorded, evaluated and remedied. The type of forum requested is similar to the one opened for the Aboriginal peoples in Geneva. We wish that the United Nations will establish a forum within the boundaries of the United States, preferably in the state of Georgia, in the city of Atlanta.

Only a limited few so-called African-Americans are knowledgeable of their internationally protected human rights. Among those who are, the members of the Lost-Found Nation of Islam can be counted. They were organized under the leadership of the late Honorable Elijah Muhammad, and taught to reclaim their own --their human rights.

The United States' central and local governments promote such negative propaganda against the late Honorable Elijah Muhammad and the Lost-Found Nation of Islam that many so-called African-Americans, who aspire to recapture their human rights, are fearful of association with this group. They fear harassment from the society and the authorities and that they will lose the blessing of "crumbs" given them by the Anglo-American. They are unaware that they have the protection of the General Assembly's proclamation of the Universal Declaration of Human Rights.

The United States ordained slavery and forced assimilation upon captive Africans for more than 400 years. America's educational system, its socialization system, coupled today with forced assimilation, have persuaded many so-called African-Americans to believe that they are full and equal citizens of America. The United States Government wishes to persuade you and the world, today, that African-Americans are full and equal members of America's society, enjoying inalienable human rights. Their propaganda is so persuasive and effective that even some so-called African-Americans believe that the self-determination of the Anglo- American is their very own.

The Universal Declaration of Human Rights states, "disregard and contempt for human rights have resulted in barbarous acts which have outraged the conscience of mankind " America's disregard and contempt for human rights ought to be seen by the U. N. as she has dispossessed us of our culture, religion and language and forced assimilation upon us. Indeed it is barbarous, and it denies us the full enjoyment of freedom.

"Whereas," according to the Universal Declaration of Human Rights, "it is essential, if man is not to be compelled to have recourse, as a last resort, to rebellion against tyranny and oppression, that his human rights should be protected by the rule of law."

The million man march on Washington D.C., 16 October, 1995, while not falling within the class of a full blown rebellion, does evidence that the so-called African-American is emerging from the period of political domestic democratic-fictionalization. Also, evidence of a growing discontent with America's social, economic and political behavior towards African-Americans can be observed by the million woman march, which took place in Philadelphia, 25 October, 1997. In addition, further evidence of the eve of rebellion of the so-called African-American against the U.S. can be observed by the upcoming million youth march. It is planned to occur 17 September 1998 in Harlem, New York.

African-Americans have looked toward and exhausted all remedies made available by the majority government, albeit, it is viewed as the oppressor. It is necessary and desirable that now African-Americans begin to look towards the United Nations and to the international community for its technical, political and economic assistance, in advance of open arms, and organized resistance to a constituted government. America's government is, particularly in the eyes of our youth, viewed as a tyrant; and tyranny, practiced by a government or its agents, according to international law, makes that government illegitimate.

It is the belief of many, and it has been widely taught by the late Honorable Elijah Muhammad that "blood will flow in the streets of America as high as a horse's bridle." The Rodney King verdict of 29 April, 1992, ignited bloodshed in not less than ten major cities in America. But the Watts incident may more clearly illustrate the point. Only one Black male was initially killed by police officers, August of 1965 in Los Angeles, yet more than ten additional major cities in America were inflamed into rioting and demonstrations as a result. There was much bloodshed.

The United Press International reported 34 persons killed and 1000 persons injured in Los Angeles alone. As an eye witness, I am representative of the one thousand (1000) persons whose blood was shed. From the butt of a shotgun, swung by one of the hundreds of officers and military soldiers, my scalp was lacerated, my face dripped with blood. Of the thousand injuries sustained in Los Angeles during the six day period of that bloody inferno, mine was perchance the least. An incomparable holocaust is today, on the horizon. That which we have pointed you to is like unto the fever which precedes the cold, or in this instance a decisive flu.

Knowing this, cannot the U. N. open a forum for this national minority in its host country?

We pray our human rights, politically and amicably can be recaptured, our rights to self determination rectified and the damages which we have sustained be awarded in great measure in order to accomplish the cathartic cleansing mentally, emotionally, and physically of our 400 years of long-suffering.

The fate of America is hers alone. We took no part in its political architecture. We were her victims. We do not have a land which we can call our own, and our human rights are not in our possession. In the absence of our own unique political machinery, they cannot ever be because we do not govern self. America has never reinstated unto us that human right. Our destiny is to this day under the control of the Anglo-American's political machinery.

The Universal Declaration of Human Rights recognizes "it is essential to promote the development of friendly relations between nations." Here, at the U. N., nations, like people, can develop friendly relations. However, during the developmental process there must exist some measure of mutual respect for one another.

There is no question that the United States of America is well respected. On the other hand, what do African-Americans, as descendants of slaves, have or possess that would command respect from the government of the United States? This government has in the past, and still currently withholds from us possession of our human rights. Thus, having been dispossessed, we will not be a respected people unless a forum is established wherein our human rights are rectified and our injuries remedied, by some force, miracle, moral or legal intervention of the U. N.

We pray that the U.S. Government not be given the tacit approval of the U. N. to subvert the opening of a forum wherein African-American grievances can be expressed, systematically and officially recorded, evaluated and remedied.

Our prayer is for the recapture of the possession of our inalienable human rights. Moreover, we solemnly pray to be heard by the U. N. and its member States, the Supreme collective human political body, and the consummate aggregated Judge of the earth.

Thank you Professor Eide, and members of the Working Group for offering the opportunity of participation. May this intervention warrant your action.

NOTE: Available at the Secretariat: Reparations Petition for United Nations Assistance under Resolution (1503) on behalf of African- Americans in the United States of America, 1994, by Mr. Silis Muhammad.

3) Oral Statement to the Working Group on Minorities, Fourth Session May 1998, Agenda Item 3 (c)

Mr. Chairman:

My name is Ida Hakim. I am the Chief Executive of a non-governmental organization. It is an honor to be here, and I sincerely thank the Working Group on Minorities for allowing participation of N.G.O.s.

Regarding the Declaration on the Rights of Persons Belonging to National or Ethnic, Religious and Linguistic Minorities: I humbly draw your attention and the attention of the Working Group to the possibility that the Declaration does not recognize the unique problems of the National Minority that we are concerned with.

Our organization has been working primarily within the United States of America. Our area of concern is human rights violations affecting National Minorities. Of particular concern to us are the violations of the human rights of African-Americans which began with the slave trade some 400 years ago, and which continue as ongoing legacies of slavery in the United States of America. Our organization is capable of collecting evidence, conducting studies, and educating the people of the United States about human rights and the responsibility of restoration and reparations. But since many of us are from the majority population, we do not claim to be authorities on what will have to be done in order to bring about a solution to the ongoing problems.

We have been listening, instead, to the solutions that are coming from within the African-American community. As grassroots observers, we have the privilege of seeing which leaders understand the meaning of self-determination, and which leaders teach about human rights. Among a people so exploited and abused as are the African-Americans, there is need for a leader with rare humility and brotherly love. Consequently, we are very pleased to see that Mr. Sills Muhammad has made himself available to participate in this session of the Working Group. Mr. Muhammad has written and lectured for years on human rights and solutions for the problems which began with the slave trade. He is someone we would describe as a leader arising from the essence of the people.

We were especially grateful when we read the resolutions of the 1997 session of the sub-Commission on Prevention of Discrimination and Protection of Minorities, and saw the Sub-Commission's recognition of the fact that African Diaspora communities in the Americas continue to suffer from the legal, political and economic legacies of the slave trade. We noted that the Sub-Commission called upon the Working Group on Minorities to consider how it might usefully address these legacies. It is our prayer that in this session, the Working Group will find ways that the United Nations can intervene and assist African-Americans.

The importance of United Nations intervention and assistance on behalf of National Minorities has been amply demonstrated in the case of the Indigenous Peoples. We are seeing more and more instances where compensation has been made, land has been returned, and cultural and religious artifacts returned to the people from whom they were stolen. Perhaps because of the support and educational efforts of the United Nations, Indigenous Nations are reviving and passing on their language, validating their true history, and remembering and appreciating their ancestry. For them recovery seems possible. They are fortunate to have land, culture, ethnic identity, religion and language to reclaim and restore into modern times.

For them and other Minorities the Declaration is an honorable document and a necessary one. There appears to be, within the Declaration, a firm resolve to protect the interest of National Minorities, and a presumption that the National Minority will have some self identity to protect, or to return to. But the Declaration does not appear to recognize the unique problems of African- Americans. The African-American is unlike other National Minorities in that he has been a victim of complete and unrelenting destruction of his identity to the point where many victims do not even know how they have been damaged or why they suffer. This is a National Minority population whose heritage has been wiped away, and whose history goes no farther than a time period of being enslaved.

Article I, Section 1 of the Declaration tells us that "States shall protect the existence and the national or ethnic, cultural, religions and linguistic identity of minorities within their respective territories and shall encourage conditions for the promotion of that identity." The United States Government cannot possible achieve this end for its African-American population because it intentionally destroyed all remnants of the identity of its slaves and slave descendants. The Constitution of the United States, the Courts, the Legislature and the Presidents have all worked together to force the assimilation of captive, Africans into the alien European culture of the United States. From the arrival of the first slave ship until this day the captive Africans have not been self-determining as a Minority and as a Nation of People.

Today's United States Government wishes to persuade you that African-Americans are full and equal members of a mufti-cultural society .Their persuasion is so effective that even some African-Americans believe it is true. For example, whereas other Minorities in the United States feel a strong desire to advance their own cause and identify with the development of their own people, increasing numbers of African-Americans can be observed identifying themselves as "multi-cultural" rather than Black.

I ask you, how can African-Americans be full and equal members of a mufti-cultural society when the only culture they have is a post-slavery culture? They have no inherited land, no accumulated assets from their labor, they have no memory of their language, no knowledge of their relatives and ancestors, they have no knowledge of their religion. Instead they have a legacy of oppression, terrorism, poverty, anger, frustration, discrimination and deceit. The only independent help that has come to them, came through the late Honorable Elijah Muhammad. The inspired blend of religion and nationalism that he taught has sewn the seed of self- love and revitalization. Without his intervention the United States Government might have succeeded in completely assimilating, and thereby destroying the descendants of its slaves.

Once again, it is our prayer that this session of the Working Group on Minorities will mark the beginning of a change in world opinion about African-Americans. It is our prayer that the United Nations will intervene and assist in bringing about a solution for African-Americans before racial violence erupts cross the United States. And, it is our prayer that both the Majority and the Minority populations of the United States will be persuaded to work together to bring about a more just world where human rights are fully respected and truth is uplifted.

We thank the Working Group again for offering the opportunity of participation and we appreciate again the participation of Mr. Silis Muhammad on behalf of African-American people.

4) Written Statement to the Sub-Commission for the Prevention of Discrimination and Protection of Minorities 50th Session, August 1998, Agenda item 2: Question of the violation of human rights and fundamental freedoms, including policies of racial discrimination and segregation and of apartheid, in all countries, with particular reference to colonial and other dependent countries and territories: report of the Sub-Commission under Commission on Human Rights resolution 8 (XXIII)

Making reference to Sub-Commission Resolution 1997/5 on racism and racial discrimination: We would like to thank the Sub-Commission for its timely recognition of the fact that the four hundred year tragedy of plantation slavery in the Americas continues to be felt, and that African Diaspora communities in the Americas continue to suffer from the legacies of the slave trade. This resolution of the Sub-Commission gave encouragement to the so-called African-Americans in the United States of America. As a consequence, our NGO organization was able to introduce a representative of African-Americans, Mr. Silis Muhammad, to the Working Group on Minorities during their recent session in May of 1998.

Mr. Muhammad delivered a prayer to the Working Group that he had articulated some four years before in a 1503 Communication on behalf of African-Americans. His prayer was that a forum be established so that the so-called African-Americans' grievances can be expressed, systematically and officially recorded, evaluated and remedied. He asked that this forum be similar to the one established for the Aboriginal peoples in Geneva, but different in that it would be established in the U.S.A., the host country of the U.N. and the place in which 42 million descendants of enslaved Africans remain.

Recognizing that the Sub-Commission Resolution refers to plantation slavery not only in the U.S.A., but in the Americas, we ask that the Sub-Commission be conscious of the fact that African-Americans are in a unique position among Africans in the Diaspora. African-Americans did not receive the benefits of a partial or full return to self-determination or self government which began to be enjoyed by Africans throughout the Diaspora as a result of the movement towards de-colonization in the 1960's. To the contrary, in the 1960's assimilation was further forced upon the African-Americans through a civil rights movement which caused the demise of whatever independent economic and cultural recovery they had been able to achieve during the years of segregation.

For those who would argue that the civil rights movement in the U.S.A. was the will of African-Americans, it should be pointed out that an equally powerful movement toward human rights and self-determination took place at the same time. The late Honorable Elijah Muhammad, although not promoted in the media nor sanctioned by the U.S. Government, was able over 40 years to organize large numbers of African-Americans behind the concept of self reliance and self determination. Every effort was made by the

U.S. Government to destroy the independent spirit that was generated by this inspired African-American leader.

While speaking to the Working Group on Minorities, Mr. Muhammad pointed out that so-called African-Americans have suffered utter and complete destruction of their culture, language, ethnic identity, and religion. For them the United Nations protection offered to Minorities is meaningless. Because of the particular cruelty of chattel slavery in the United States, so-called African-Americans were able to retain nothing of their past and of their homelands. Hence, the truth arises... that unlike some of the Africans in the Diaspora, who do retain remnants of their original culture and identity, African-Americans possess no remnants, and therefore must build their future from nothing but their own will to survive slavery. Thus the vast majority are in the condition of a lost people whose assimilation has been so complete that they cannot identify what they suffer from.

A special issue of the American magazine Newsweek reported that slavery and racism are comparable to the "chicken and the egg." They concluded that the most malign legacy of slavery is racism. We agree that racism is a legacy of slavery. But we feel that along with many other legacies, it is but a symptom of the far greater problem. The right to self-determination has always been denied African- Americans throughout their 443 year history in the Americas, including 222 years of being subject to the will of the U.S. Government. We ask: If African-Americans had ever been allowed, assisted or encouraged in their efforts toward self determination, would they now be subject to what is perhaps the most virulent racism in the earth?

We believe that if the U.N. will establish a forum for African-Americans in the United States, through that act alone

African-Americans will begin to fully understand that the Nations of the earth wish to help them recapture their rights as human beings. We believe that by doing this, an upcoming race war, or racial violence may be averted. We join Mr. Muhammad in his prayer for a forum and we encourage the Sub-Commission to act upon his prayer quickly. As a recent hate crime in Texas should demonstrate (the crime wherein a Black man was abducted by three white men and was dragged behind a pick-up truck until his head was torn from his body), the potential for an eruption of racial violence in the U.S. is greater by the day and by the hour.

We have taken notice of Resolution 1998/26 of the Commission on Human Rights regarding the upcoming World Conference Against Racial Discrimination, Xenophobia and Related Intolerance. We see that the Commission on Human Rights has invited the Sub-Commission to carry out preparatory studies without delay, and to transmit its recommendations to the Commission and to the Preparatory Committee. The Commission on Human Rights also asked for the recommendations of specialized agencies of the U.N., and the full participation of NGO's. We are responding to the call, and are prepared to be involved in the preparatory process for this world conference. As a first step we would suggest that studies be undertaken which would serve to evaluate the damage done to the African-American people.

Two areas that our organization has pinpointed as especially in need of study are:

1) The lingering effects of plantation slavery, terrorism and racial discrimination on the present day physical and psychological health of African-Americans: We want studies specific to African-Americans and related to chattel slavery.

There is a great deal of information available on the subject, and some enlightening research has been done, but there exists no comprehensive analysis or conclusion as to damage.

2) The criminalization of the African-American: There is broad based agreement in the African- American legal community that the U.S. legislature and State legislatures have passed racially discriminatory laws which target African-Americans. These laws have resulted in the rapid rise in incarceration rates and rapid growth of a private prison industry .The sad fact is that young Black men are now more valuable to the U.S. economy in prison than out. In prison many of them are put to work manufacturing products for private corporations. The criminalization of the African-American may soon be recognized as the resurrection of slavery in the United States.

We are confident that any studies undertaken by the Sub-Commission or by specialized agencies of the U.N. will serve to verify the need for a forum for African-Americans.

We cannot express strongly enough the need for action in response to the prayer of Mr. Silis Muhammad. We also cannot express strongly enough the need for the independence of a U.N. forum and the independence of U.N. sponsored studies. We pray that the U.S. Government may not be given the tacit approval of the U.N. to undermine the efforts that Mr. Muhammad is making on behalf of African-Americans.

We continue to stress that when evaluating racism in the United States, African-Americans should be studied within their own category. We assert that the racism directed against African-Americans is not comparable with that directed against other people of color in the U. S. or ethnic or religious minorities in the U.S. There is a question as to whether or not African-Americans even fit within the category of minority.

Therefore we stress that African-Americans should be viewed separately for the following reasons: 1) because of the evidence that they do not fit the category of minority. (In his closing statements to the Working Group on Minorities, the Chairman, Professor Eide, did offer words to the effect that thought must be directed toward the problem of African-Americans not fitting the category of minority, and the question of where they do fit.) 2) because of the long time period of their oppression, the brutality of their experience, the damages which have been inflicted, and the fact that they have not received any remuneration nor have they been assisted in attaining any degree of repair (their culture, religion, language and land) as like other Africans who suffer the legacies of plantation slavery; and 3) because of the well documented history of U.S. Government subversive action taken against the grassroots movements of African-Americans, and manipulation of their collective will through the media.

With appreciation for the efforts of the United Nations to see that justice is done in the earth, we again thank the Sub-Commission for the Prevention of Discrimination and Protection of Minorities for its attention directed toward the legacies of the slave trade.

5) Oral Statement to the Sub-Commission for the Prevention of Discrimination and Protection of Minorities
August 1998, 50th Session, Agenda Item 2

Greetings Mr. Chairman, Members of the Sub-Commission, Delegates, Staff members, NGOs and guests: My name is Silis Muhammad. I am a spiritual son of the late Honorable

Elijah Muhammad (peace be upon him). Oh! How much he did for us, the so-called African-Americans, and perchance, too, for humanity.

Our issue is the violation of human rights and fundamental freedoms. When we consider Article 27 of the International Covenant on Civil and Political Rights, which the United States of America has ratified, we conclude that we, the descendants of slaves (the so-called African-Americans), remain a lost people. We are dislodged from the knowledge of our cultural beginning. We remain dislodged from the knowledge of our ancestral tradition of religion. Regarding our language, as slaves we were by force prevented from speaking it, and we are lost still from the use of it.

We, particularly in the United States, live under a system of forced assimilation within the ruling culture.

Thus, to the extent that we have been deprived of our culture, our religion and our language, we do not have inalienable human rights. Is that not a question for the United Nations to resolve, or to take part in the resolution on We are lost still, as a result of the lingering effects of plantation slavery.

We have returned to Geneva to request the assistance of the Sub-Commission in the establishment of a forum to address the question of reclaiming our original human rights, or deciding upon whether we choose to assimilate, for upon this matter we have never enjoyed the freedom of choice.

Having been dispossessed of those inherent rights, possessed by every minority (and protected by the United Nations), we believe that through a forum we can define ourselves, thereby assisting the United Nations in fulfilling its most honorable covenant with the human families and peoples of the earth, as at present, we are left out.

We would ask that our decisions be officially recorded and our prayers for reconstruction heard. Once we have declared our inalienable rights, as only we can, we would pray to the United Nations to recognize those rights sculptured by our own hands. We ask for the forum to be established at the United Nations in New York, under the auspices of the Sub-Commission.

Furthermore, we suggest that if the more acute problems evidenced in the United States can be successfully addressed within a forum, then the problems of all of the Diaspora communities can be explored more efficaciously by the creation of a new Working Group in Geneva.

The General Assembly proclaims that recognition of the inherent dignity and of the equal and inalienable rights of all members of the human family is the foundation of freedom, justice and peace in the world. Here, to the extent that we have been dispossessed of our equal and inalienable rights, and uprooted from any inherent ancestral dignity, we are absent full and complete freedom, justice and equality in the world. Thereby, all of the Americas and potentially Europe, along with ourselves, are absent the very foundation of peace.

Our youth embody the wrath of the transmissible effects of plantation slavery. Their disposition is expressed in their "rap" music. Oftentimes contained in the lyrics are the very words "No justice! No peace!"

My presence here is axiomatic of unfolding history. A potential holocaust is today on the horizon, particularly, in the United States of America. Will the United Nations persuade her to let my people go?

We thank you, members of the Sub-Commission, for your attention and your consideration. May this intervention warrant your actions.

Written Statement to the UN in 1997

The following statement was sent to the UN as the first communication of CURE/AFRE.

Written Statement to the 49th Session on the Prevention of Discrimination and the Protection of Minorities
CURE/AFRE

1. Making reference to the report of Special Rapporteur, Mr. Maurice Glele-Ahanhanzo, on his mission to the United States of America in 1994 (document E/CN.4/1995/78/Add.l.): In this report the Special Rapporteur accurately informs the Economic and Social Council that the human rights of African Americans have been violated from the establishment of the United States until the present day. However, the Special Rapporteur states that racism may not now be a deliberate policy on the part of the U.S. Government. We seek to inform the United Nations that the report did not express the bitterness of the African American people and their sincere belief that racial discrimination is a deliberate policy. Because of the exhaustion of domestic remedy, there now exists a belief that racial discrimination will never cease. This belief is confirmed by the failure of African American leaders in the U.S. Congress to gain permission from the Caucasian majority for a mere study of slavery to determine whether reparations are due.

2. In 1993 a highly respected African American leader delivered a 1503 communication to the Working Group on

Communications on behalf of African Americans. This communication, delivered by the Honorable Silis Muhammad, leader of the Lost Found Nation of Islam, was not forwarded to the Sub-Commission because it did not prove a consistent pattern of human rights violations. We believe the United Nations knows that a consistent pattern of human rights violations is already a matter of African, European and American history, brought up to the present and verified by the aforementioned Special Rapporteur. The African American population is becoming aware that their 1503 communication was rejected by the Working Group and therefore ignored by the United Nations. This awareness adds to the already existing belief that racial discrimination will never cease.

3. Making reference to the recent remarks of U.S. President Bill Clinton wherein he mentions the possibility of an apology for slavery, we seek to inform the United Nations that the masses of African Americans feel that an apology is not enough, while the masses of Caucasian Americans feel there is no reason to apologize. In monitoring the African American press and internet communications, we have observed that African Americans do not believe President Clinton has the interest of justice at heart. African Americans have seen the U.S. government strike down Affirmative Action and special preferences in universities and law schools, some of which now have 100% Caucasian enrollment. They have also seen that the U.S. Judicial System continues to imprison African American men at 10 times the rate of Caucasian men and execute the death penalty at the same rate. Now, after President Clinton's remarks, they see that Caucasian Americans can conceive of no reason to even apologize for slavery.

4. The prayers of African Americans for justice and reparations have been rejected by the U.S. Government and, seemingly, the United Nations. Because the struggle seems hopeless, the African American population has reached a state of extreme anxiety .We observe that some leaders are considering changing their tactics because of the failure of peaceful and legal means of solving the problem. We believe that African Americans may decide to use extreme measures and thereby gain the attention of the world community .We fear that the U.S. Government may respond with imprisonment of African American leaders. We ask the U.N. to respond to our communication by establishing a meeting wherein African American Leaders (those who are not under the authority of the U.S. Government) can speak to the UN Human Rights authorities candidly and privately about the desperate plight of African Americans.

Petition for Reparations to the UN under 1503 Procedure delivered in 1994

The 1503 Petition for Reparations for African Americans was delivered to the UN in 1994. Although it was received, it was not heard nor was it responded to by the UN.

PREFACE

We, the African descendants of slaves, the so-called African-American, the so-called Black American, the so-called Negro, have never tasted of the "freedom" that so many millions of other members of the human family enjoy, safeguard and treasure. We are the only people on this planet that have had to endure over four hundred (400) years of the most brutal, dehumanizing slavery the world has ever known. We continue to suffer to this day from the scars of that slavery and from institutions of racism in the United States of America that deprive us of our "human rights."

This historic Petition to the United Nations marks an end of one era and beginning of another. It marks the end of the struggle for liberty that many Black Americans have fought within the boundaries of the United States in an attempt to get our former slave masters to give us what we were born with, our human rights.

We, as a people, have survived the post-civil war when we were released from the physical chains and told to "go" with little or no assistance from the United States Government. We even survived the violent and frightening reign of terror of the Klu Klux Klan and the White Citizens Councils. During the years of the Great Depression, we suffered the most.

During World War II, Black soldiers were placed on the front lines to defend a nation that inflicted insults of the worst kind upon them, their families and loved ones who sought to exercise their human rights in places of public accommodations and in the work place.

We have had many great leaders during this era--leaders who begged and pleaded to the government and to the white majority Americans, to do what is right and just. Among those, to name a few, have been: Harriet Tubman, Frederick Douglas, Sojourner Truth, and Booker T. Washington.

The push for civil rights in the sixties brought us into a period wherein we experienced an even more cruel fate. We were led to believe that integration would be a "cure-all" for our woes. With integration we were to be able to experience life in these United States as do the majority of white Americans. Several decades into this system of "forced assimilation" reveals that the "glass ceiling" will continue to block the majority of us from ever truly "arriving." Our great leaders--Thurgood Marshall, Martin Luther King, Jr., Ralph Abernathy--proponents of integration, did not intend to dedicate their life's works to a system that would still manage to keep us under control. But under control we still are.

We have had several great leaders with the wisdom to see that in order to be truly free, we must be able to exercise ALL of the rights that citizens of other nations exercise. We must have the right to self-determination which includes the right to: decide our own destiny, study and perpetuate our own history, culture and languages; have real political power in determining and electing officials that will be able to protect rights and needs peculiar to African-Americans; and even to return to Mother Africa, with substance, in order to undo the damages of slavery. Among these leaders were W.E.B. DuBois, Marcus Garvey, the Honorable Elijah Muhammad and Malcolm X.

We now are at the beginning of a new era wherein we now will take our struggle for true and complete freedom to the international community via the United Nations. Our leader in this arena is the Honorable Silis Muhammad, my husband, who has dedicated his life's work in carrying out the mission of his leader and teacher, the Honorable Elijah Muhammad. He is working day and night to enable African-Americans to sit down as equals with officials of the government of the United States in a forum governed by the United Nations, so that this government will have to answer for its systematic and continuous gross violations of our human rights protected under international law.

So great is his love for his people that he has placed his life on the line in order to ensure that African-Americans are afforded the right to self-determination, and to receive justice in the form of reparations. I, along with countless others, pledge, my love and loyalty to him in this great and historic endeavor! Those of us in this spiritual battle are warriors, and are reminded of the sayings of the prophet Isaiah:

"For every battle of the warrior is with

Confused noise and garments rolled in blood;

But **this** shall be with burning **and** fuel of fire.

The Bible, Isaiah,

Chapter 9, Verse 5

Misshaki Muhammad

Attorney General of the

Lost-Found Nation of Islam

Atlanta, Georgia

Reparations Petition for United Nations assistance under

Resolution 1503 on behalf of African-Americans in the United States of America

Ref. N. G/SO 215/1 USA (266)

Mr. Boutros Boutros-Ghali

Secretary-General of the United Nations

Palais des Nations

United Nations

CH-1211 Geneva

Switzerland

Re: The past and present gross violations of the human rights of the African-American people to self determination by means of official U.S. policies of slavery, segregation, and forced assimilation, and the refusal of the U.S. government to apologize and offer any compensation, or reparations for these violations.

Whereas recognition of the inherent dignity and of the equal and inalienable rights of all members of the human family is the foundation of freedom, justice and peace in the world;

Whereas both the fundamental rights of members of minorities to exist in equal status with the majority, as well as the historical oppression and resulting present inequality and circumstances of the African-Americans (descendants of the formerly enslaved Africans in the U.S.) are well known;

Keeping in mind that Articles 1 and 55 of the U.N. Charter specifically refer to the principle of self-determination; that one of the basic purposes of the U.N., according to Article 1(2) is to,...develop friendly relations among nations based on respect for the principle of equal rights and self-determination of peoples ...;" that Article 55 explicitly ties the principle of self-determination to respect for human rights and fundamental freedoms for all or part of its people; that the principle of self-determination is implicated in chapters XI, XII and XIII of the Charter, that in the years since 1945, the principle has found its way into both the International Covenants, the Declaration of the Granting of Independence to Colonial Countries and Peoples, the Declaration of Principles of International Law Concerning Friendly Relations, the Declaration on the Rights of Indigenous Peoples, and the decisions of the International Court of Justice in its advisory opinions in the Namibia and Western Sahara cases, just as it has been upheld by the U.N. General Assembly in relation to numerous recently emerging eastern European nations; and that, although long applied only in the colonial context, it has increasingly been appealed to in the post-colonial age by minorities and secessionist movements to the extent that today legal scholars--even (as before suggested) the U.N. itself--have generally agreed that the principle of self-determination may well apply outside of the colonial context, though within strict limits;

Keeping in mind that Articles 1 and 55 of the Charter commit the U.N. to the promotion of universal respect for human rights and basic freedoms, while Article 56 gives member nations an obligation to act, jointly or separately, to achieve the purposes set out in Article 55--that is, Article 56 creates a duty to act to promote respect for rights and freedoms,; and that when the core human rights rooted in the principle of autonomy are grossly, systematically and persistently violated, U.N. intervention to end that violation is morally and legally permissible, since the principle of autonomy implies that government is only justifiable if the government and its policies are an expression of the self-determination of peoples;

Realizing that today there can be little doubt that nations which practice, encourage or condone activities such as genocide, ethnocide, ethnic cleansing, forced assimilation, systematic racial discrimination, etc, are in violation of international law;

Recognizing that of such violations, only those that are (1) persistent and (2) systematic will be sufficiently severe or gross as to justify U. N. involvement; and that violations are systematic if they are a part of a consistent pattern, or a matter of state policy (systematic violations include both overt governmental actions or covert but institutionalized practices, the effect of which is to regularly prevent the exercise of core rights, and are more than occasional, or of short duration (e.g., U.S.slavery, segregation, systemic racial discrimination);

Understanding that to be a people, a group of persons must not only subjectively see themselves as a single people, but also objectively be seen, through speech and action, to be participating or be able to participate in the creation or recreation of their own distinct social world.

Recognizing that the legal acceptability of self-determination outside of the colonial context also means making a distinction between external and internal self-determination; that is, limiting self-determination to minority rights as it has been interpreted under Article 27 of the ICCPR, and evolved in customary international law;

Recognizing that just as a gross systemic and persistent denial of human rights is a violation of international law, calling forth the right to international assistance, the violation of the human right to internal self-determination and reparations as permitted in minority rights--that is the concentration of all the power of a multi-national state in the hands of a single group within it which acts to prevent other constituent peoples from realizing their own social, historical and cultural space--is equally a violation of international law, calling forth the right to receive U.N. assistance. Any government or the agents and institutions of the government that, in principle, prevent the exercise of a people's right to self-determination, and compensation for past and present gross violations, or any other minority rights, may be regarded as illegitimate in the eyes of that people, and by international law in its application to that people, insofar as U.N. efforts to give a voice to the people is called for in principle.

Further recognizing, in regard to reparations for past gross violations, that the right to a remedy for victims of gross violation of human rights is well-established, and involves reparations, which include compensation, restitution or restoration. Concerning this fundamental international legal principle, the Permanent Court of International Justice ruled in the Chorzow Factory (indemnity) Case:

> It is a principle of international law, and even a general conception of law, that any breach of an agreement invokes an obligation to make reparation.... reparation is the indispensable complement of a failure to apply a convention, and there is no necessity for this to be stated in the convention itself.

Drawing attention to the pertinence of a number of both universal and regional human rights instruments containing express provisions relating to the right to an "effective remedy" by competent national tribunals for acts violating human rights (see Article 8 of the Universal Declaration of Human Right). The notion of an "effective remedy" is also included in Article 2(3) of the International Covenant on Civil and Political Rights, and in Article 6 of the Declaration on the Elimination of All Forms of Racial Discrimination. Some human rights instruments refer to a more particular "rights to be compensated in accordance with the law" or the "right to an adequate compensation." Even more specific are the provisions of Article 9(5) of the International Covenant on Civil and Political Rights, and of Article 5(5) of the European Convention for the Protection of Human Rights and Fundamental Freedoms, which refer to the "enforceable right to compensation." Similarly, the Convention Against Torture and Other Cruel, Inhuman or Degrading Treatment or Punishment contains a provision providing for the torture victim a redress and "an enforceable right to fair and adequate compensation, including the means for as full rehabilitation as possible." In some instruments, a specific provision is contained indicating that compensation is due in accordance with law or with national law. Equally, provisions relating to "reparation" or "satisfaction" of damages are contained in the International Convention on the Elimination of All Forms of Racial Discrimination. Article 6, which provides for the right to seek "just and adequate reparation or satisfaction for any damage suffered." The ILO Convention concerning Indigenous and Tribal Peoples in Independent Countries also refers to "fair compensation for damages," to "compensation in money" and "under appropriate guarantees." And all to full compensation "for any loss or injury." The American Convention on Human Rights, to which the U.S. is a party, speaks of "compensatory damages" (Article 68) and provides that the consequences of the measure or situation that constituted the breach of the right or freedom "be remedied" and the "fair compensation be paid to the injured party." The Convention on the Rights of the Child contains a provision to the effect that states Parties shall take all appropriate measures to promote "physical and psychological recovery and social reintegration of a child victim..." In short, numerous human rights instruments provide strong evidence that the right to remedy is an established obligation where states' action or failure to act result in damages.

Bearing in mind, concerning the issue as to whether the internationally accepted obligation to remedy is applicable to damages suffered by minorities due to past gross violation of human rights, that Sub-Commission resolution 1989/14 provides our first useful guidance as to victims rights to reparation. The resolution mentions in its first preambular paragraph "individuals, groups and communities". This supports our assumption that the right to remedy deals with minorities as well as individuals. That minorities are included is also confirmed in Sub-Commission resolution 1988/11 of 1 September 1988 which, in its first operative paragraph, refers to "victims", either individually or collectively." Another indication regarding the categories of victims is the repeated reference in Sub-Commission resolution 1989/14 to "gross violations of human rights and fundamental freedoms." Under most international legal instruments dealing with individual rights, the violation of any one provision may entail a right to an appropriate remedy, while instruments concerned with the rights of minorities to Compensation focus on gross violations of human rights and fundamental freedoms.

Drawing particular attention to the fact that according to the domestic law of the U.S. itself (Third Restatement of the Foreign Relations Law of the United State), a state violates international law if, as a matter of State policy, it practices, encourages or condones:

(a) genocide

(b) slavery or slave trade

(c) the murder or causing the disappearance of individuals

(d) torture or other cruel, inhuman or degrading treatment or punishment

(e) prolonged arbitrary detention

(f) systematize racial discrimination, or

(g) a consistent pattern of gross violations of internationally recognized human rights.

Affirming the general recognition that victims who are entitled to compensation--and this may also include their descendants or survivors--have suffered substantial damages and harm. This interpretation is reflected in the first preambular paragraph of Sub-Commission resolution 1989/14 which refers to "substantial damages and acute sufferings." In this regard the notion of "victims" spelled out in paragraph 18 of the Declaration of Basic Principles of Justice for Victims of Crime and Abuse of Power, should be taken into account. The paragraphs reads in part:

> "Victims means persons who individually or collectively, have suffered harm, including physical or mental injury, emotional suffering, economic loss or substantial impairment of their fundamental rights, through acts or omissions that ...constitute violations... of internationally recognized norms relating to human rights.)

And further recognizing that for the many African-Americans whose ancestors were victims of gross violations, passage of time has no attenuating effect, but on the contrary has increased post-traumatic stress, deteriorated social, material, etc., conditions requiring all necessary special rights as well as compensation and rehabilitation measures. We may conclude that as long as the effects of past gross violation and resulting damage can be demonstrated as the cause of present developmental problems, it would be difficult to produce an acceptable argument for statutory limitations since that would amount to the denial of the fundamental human right to a remedy for past injustices. Therefore, in concern for future generations and our search for an end to war and violence, we must uphold human rights for African-Americans, because in this era of scattered low-intensity violent conflicts, only justice can effectively supersede war.

Remembering that the Permanent Court of International Justice establishes the basic principles governing remedy for breaches of international obligation, stating:

> The essential principle contained in the actual notion of an illegal act--a principle which seems to be established by international practice and in particular by the decisions of arbitral tribunals--is that reparation must, as far as possible, wipe out all consequences of the illegal act and reestablish the

situation which would, in all probability, have existed, if that act had not been committed. Restitution in kind or, if this is not possible, payment of sum corresponding to the value which a restitution in kind would bear, the award, if need be, of damages for loss sustained which would not be covered by restitution in kind or payment in place of it--such are the principles which should serve to determine the amount of compensation due for an act contrary to international law.

In full consideration of all of the above, we believe that the African-American people suffer from gross, systematic and persistent violation of their human rights, particularly their right to self-determination and right to remedy for past and ongoing gross human rights violation, and therefore the following petition is prepared by The Lost-Found Nation of Islam, on behalf of African-Americans, to call forth the assistance of the U.N. and the international community:

Dear Mr. Boutros-Boutros Ghali and Members of the Sub-Commission:

(Fatma Zahra, Farida Alouaze, Ahmed Khalifa, Ahmed Khalil, Fisseha Yirner, Hailma Embarek Wazazi, Judith Sell Attah, El Hadji Guisse', Said Maceur Ramadhane, Tofazzol Hassain Khan, Jin Tian, Muksum-Ul-Hakim, Ribat Hatano, Awn Shawkat Al-Khasawneh, Ioan Maxim, Stanislav Valentinovich Chernnichenko, Volodymyr Boutkevitch, Leandro Despouy, Giberto Vergre Saboia, Clemencai Forero Ucros, Miguel Alfonso Martinez, Claude Heller, Marc Bossuyt, Louis Joint, Erica-Irene A. Daes, Asbjorn Eide, Claire Palley, and Linda Chavez)

The Lost-Found Nation of Islam (hereinafter referred to as The Nation of Islam), under the leadership and guidance of the Honorable Silis Muhammad, on behalf of its members and all other descendants of enslaved Africans in America, takes this opportunity to congratulate and thank the Working Group of the

Sub-Commission and those members who voted to accept for consideration the IHRAAM Petition of 30 April 1992 concerning Los Angeles motorist Rodney King, in the context of past and present gross violations of human rights of African-Americans in the U.S. Although the petition was narrowly defeated in the Sub-Commission, the Nation of Islam was delighted to see that, so shortly after the show of international concern by the Working Group and many members of the Sub-Commission, the U.S. saw fit to ratify the International Covenant on Civil and Political Rights (ICCPR), to bring a new black Ambassador to the U.N., to find new legal grounds to retry the police involved in the cruel and callous beating of the African-American motorist, Rodney King, and to effectively prosecute the Detroit police (See Appendix A) for the murder of an African American, Malice Green.

While it cannot be directly linked, some African-American organizations, such as those represented by The Nation of Islam or cooperating actively with The Nation of Islam feel that the concern shown by the Sub-Commission may have been instrumental in securing a fair verdict in the King and Green trials, which thus discouraged new rounds of violence, loss of life, and property damage. If this is true, the U.S. government and all Americans should be thankful to the Sub-Commission for showing the degree of concern it did.

However, while it is likely that national and international opinion probably encouraged the jury conviction of the officers in the King trial, the minimal sentence of 30 months that Judge Davies imposed upon them, his refusal to impose any fines (where $250,000.00 in fines had been pending), and his assignment of part of the blame to the victim, Mr. King, for the treatment that he endured, all indicate that the historic difficulty of African-Americans in obtaining justice through U.S. courts persists. (See Derrick Bell for a listing of major cases in which African-American interest was surrendered to that of the Anglo-American majority, Appendix B; also see Aviam Soifer and Kathleen M. Sullivan for restrictions placed upon justiciable discrimination by recent rulings in U.S. Courts, Appendix C).

Dear Members of the Sub-Commission,

In situations of historical gross violations of human rights without reparations or compensation, the individual cases are only single manifestations of the larger phenomenon of general disrespect for the human rights of a formerly enslaved, powerless, dominated and exploited minority. As you know, the history of Africans in America began with the capture and forced emigration of African populations. During the "middle voyage" to America and the enslavement which awaited survivors, millions met their deaths. While scholars estimate that some 15 million Africans were landed alive on North America, estimates of the numbers lost or killed in the slave trade have ranged as high as 100 million souls. The social fabric of an entire civilization was rent and destroyed in the process. The African population did not ask to come to America-- their arrival was purely involuntary and against their will, and for the purpose of exploitation of their labor (See The African Slave Trade, Appendix D).

In order to justify the enormity of this crime against humanity, the Anglo-American government, slave masters, and majority population were forced to attempt to regard the African population as mere property and less than human. This entailed a refusal to admit their cultures, and effort to destroy their social habits and the long and rich traditions which they carried with them from the land of their birth, by labeling these barbaric and heathen. For example, any African caught practicing Islam was mercilessly tortured, killed, or forced to go into hiding. The use of African names and African languages was widely prohibited. The official U.S. policy of forced assimilation (referred to in the U.S. as "integration," despite its incongruousness with customary usage of that term) actually began during the enslavement period with the concerted efforts to stamp out any use or recognition of the African cultural heritage in America. This aspect of official policy was to be sufficiently successful in the areas of language and religion as to produce, from the many African cultures, a new one: African-Americans.

Subsequent to the Civil War, American citizenship was conferred upon the descendants of the enslaved Africans without any pretense of democratic consultation. While the government of Abraham Lincoln made numerous promises in order to secure the effective African-American support against the forces of the southern Confederacy, these promises were only briefly instituted in the Reconstruction period following the Civil War. Shortly thereafter, African-Americans were forced into a system of "separate" but equal segregation, which they rejected insofar as the "separate' was not self-administered, and the "equal" was not equally resourced. In short, "separate" meant political, cultural and economic domination with segregation. During this period, they struggled against discriminatory Jim Crow laws, which limited their participation in society at every conceivable level, including use of public lavatories, and seating in public transportation. Ironically, it was during this period of segregation that the recognition of African-American ethnic difference formed a theoretical cornerstone of the Anglo-American government's justification of the policy of apartheid, even though the government had no intention of providing minority rights, or the right to be different, in any egalitarian sense. The official policy of "separate but equal" in reality was intended to serve a societal opiate to contain African-American revolt, and secure co-operation; it did not provide for any significant economic or political equality or autonomy. However, the separate but equal period, like the period preceding it, permitted, or was unable to prevent, the welding of separate African traditions into what became a distinct and recognizable African-American culture, demonstrable in lifestyle, music, cuisine, dress, language, dance, religious practice, socio-political organization, and a wide range of distinct cultural attributes which distinguish the African-American people from the majority population--even though the eventual commercialization and distortion of much of African-Americans' cultural products did much to disguise the unique nature of the culture.

The policy of forced assimilation moved toward a final stage in the 1960's, following the massive struggle by the African-American

Islam feels and historical evidence substantiates (see Appendix H), until African-Americans are able to exercise their right to self-determination and receive reparations for past and on-going gross human rights violations. The Nation of Islam and most African-Americans believe that this will require third party intervention, such as the U.N. Sub-Commission's willingness to provide the political, legal and conceptual leverage, the fora and the legal framework required by the oppressed formerly enslaved minority to convince the U.S. government to open a sincere dialogue on the inalienable human rights of the minority to lawfully demand self-determination with reparations for past and on-going gross human rights violations--chiefly, the receipt of compensation for past and on-going gross violation to the full extent necessary to achieve self-determination and minority rights as provided by Article 27 of the International Covenant on Civil and Political Rights, which the U.S. has ratified.

Mr. Secretary-General and Members of the Sub-Commission:

The U.S. government, in line with the U.S. Courts, continues to promote forced assimilation through the concept that all minority needs and rights can be subsumed within the concept of non-discrimination and equality (or sameness) before the law--this despite the fact that historical evidence strongly contradicts such a notion, and that judicial enforcement of non-discrimination in the U.S. has become formal and de-contextualized, disallowing appropriate consideration for historical injustices and present special needs. The courts further restrict satisfaction by requiring "intent to discriminate," and refusing consideration to those who are not "immediate victims" (See Soifer and Sullivan, Appendix 3)

The rectification of profound damages caused by past and present U.S. systemic discrimination against and gross violation of the human rights of African-Americans cannot occur until African-Americans are able to exercise their minority rights. All statistical evidence (Appendix H) indicates that a policy of non-discrimination alone is insufficient to permit the African-American minority to achieve equal status with the majority, but rather, under the guise of aiding them, serves to continue their victimization. While a multi-national state may argue that treating all people (majority as well as formerly enslaved minority) the same, legally and institutionally, regardless of their different histories and circumstances, somehow leads to a new society in which oppressed or formerly enslaved minorities, at some time in the future, will achieve equal-status, sameness or equality with the majority, this line of reasoning more frequently serves merely to justify or mask majority domination, and often exploitation, of national minorities. Even the most superficial analysis reveals that treating such minorities as if they were the same as the majority in a majority-ruled multi-national society does not permit minority needs to be legitimately known or expressed, let alone addressed. Practically every multi-national society since the dawn of written history tried some version of this notion without succeeding, usually with the implicit intention of maintaining the domination of the minority group. That is why every U.N. study on minorities, such as those of Cruz, Capotorit, Eide, Calley, Daes, etc., discovered that non-discrimination may not be enough, and special measures or special rights are often required by Article 2:2 in conjunction with Article 27 of the ICCPR to achieve equal status for national minorities. These special rights often include various forms of autonomy (self-determination) such as that requested during a thirty-five (35) year period for African Americans by the Honorable Elijah Muhammad, founder of the Nation of Islam.

In relation to this issue, Karel Vasak suggested in the *International Dimension of Human Rights* that without self-determination, (internal and external) all other rights become meaningless. Similarly, unless African-Americans are accorded appropriate forms of internal self-determination, it may not be possible for them to experience their human rights. Further, without appropriate enablement (reparations) provided over time to financially facilitate the development required to exercise self-determination, to facilitate the establishment of minority policies and institutions, the right to experience human rights will not be achieved.

Mr. Secretary-General and Sub-Commission Members,

The United States has refused to respond adequately to its obligation to provide African-Americans with either minority rights (which may require varying degrees of internal self-determination) or compensation for past gross human rights violations.

A current example of refusal of the U.S. government to address these two related issues is the case of Lani Guinier, who was nominated as Assistant Attorney General for Civil Rights with the support of the African-American community. Ms. Guinier's modest proposal of "modified at-large voting," described by some as "an eloquent plea against electoral quotas," nonetheless created a furor in the business community, which vilified it as representing a form of affirmative action (See Appendix I). Ms. Guinier's nomination was then rescinded by President Bill Clinton, despite the pertinence of the following issues:

> 1) The right of African-Americans to effective participation in the democratic process is provided for in Articles 2:2, 2:3 and 5 of the U. N. Declaration on the Rights of National or Ethnic, Religious and Linguistic Minorities, which is widely viewed as a further elaboration of the rights of minorities provided for in Article 27 of the International covenant on Civil and Political Rights. The American electoral system is so structured as to prevent African-Americans from having anything to say about their elected leadership. Under this system, they are discouraged from democratically electing the leadership of their community. They must always leave the election of their community leaders in the control of the Anglo-American majority. The principle of majority rule is used on the federal and state levels, rather than any of a number of systems of proportional representation, widely recognized for their capacity to reelect minority interest. On the municipal level, the "at large" voting system which has largely replaced the

Ward system in American cities has been employed to effectively reduce African-American electoral influence. There are no special institutionalized procedures for democratic determination or effective exercise of African-American opinion.

2) The right to affirmative action (special measures) was provided for explicitly by Article 2:2 and implicitly by Article 27 of the International Covenant on Civil and Political Rights (ICCPR), as well as by Articles 1:4 and 2:2 of the Convention on the Elimination of All forms of Racial Discrimination (CERD), and 4:2 of the Declaration on Minorities. In addition to its ratification of the ICCPR, the U. S. is also guided by the Restatement (Third) of the Foreign Relations Law of the U. S., which details it obligations to observe treaty and customary international law.

The willingness of the highest executive authority in the United States, President Clinton, to respond to putative fears of affirmative action rather than uphold it in accordance with his international-legal obligations under the ICCPR constitutes yet another indication of U.S. policymakers' historic tendency to block initiatives arising from the African-American community to address their political and socio-economic interest, in favor of the interest of powerful sectors of the dominant majority (See Y.N. Kly, *International Law and the Black Minority in the U.S.*, 1985). Indeed, it is a refusal to permit African-Americans to experience a democratic process in the choice of their leaders and/or their community policies, if these leaders or policies do not accord with the interest of the Anglo-American majority--even if the majority's interest involves enslavement or apartheid (segregation) for the African-American, as it admittedly has in the past, or absorption into the American "underclass" through the processes of forced assimilation, which is primarily the U.S. policy regarding African-Americans in the present. Following this historical pattern, certainly the day after tomorrow for African-Americans will be the same as the day before yesterday.

Mr. Secretary-General and Members of the Sub-Commission,

American jurisprudence, like that of most states, recognizes the right of victims to remedy. It has generally acknowledged that individuals may be entitled to compensation for the effects of actions wrongfully undertaken even before those harmed were born. Furthermore, such acknowledgement has occurred not only on an individual basis, but on a collective basis. When the U. S. Congress has exercised its authority under Section 2 of the Thirteenth Amendment and Section 5 of the Fourteenth Amendment--Amendments whose original intent was for the protection of formerly enslaved African-Americans--it has done so to protect groups or classes of persons, not to serve individual interests. The Congress is addressing the institution and legacy of slavery as an ancient wrong and redressing grievances of those presently affected by establishing modern rights.

U. S. Recognition of the collective right to remedy is reflected in the U.S. payment of reparations to the Sioux of South Dakota (1985), the Seminoles of Florida (1985), the Ottawas of Michigan (1986) and Japanese Americans (1990). A similar recognition exists in the international community, where we note the payment of reparations to the Jewish people by Germany in 1952, to Japanese Canadians by Canada in 1988, and to Holocaust survivors by Austria in 1990.

Concerning the right to reparations for gross human rights violations of African-Americans, the Nation of Islam challenges the hypocritical manipulation of affirmative action by the U.S. government which:

> a) seeks to represent those affirmative action programs which it instituted subsequent to the African-American insurrections of the 1960's as compensation for past gross human rights violations

of African-Americans through official policies of enslavement and segregation, while at the same time failing to officially admit to and apologize for such policies;

b) purports to be the sole determinant of what such compensations should be--*i.e.*, to offer compensation for grievances without any consultation or negotiation with the descendants of the African-American victims, whose communities continue to suffer from the malaise engendered by such policies, as to their preferred mode of compensation.

c) having decided to compensate the African-Americans without officially consulting them, apologizing or admitting wrong-doing, the U.S. majority's institutions then proceed to unilaterally rescind and dismantle affirmative action, the very mode of reparations that the U.S. credits itself for having offered as a remedy.

Mr. Secretary-General and Sub-Commission Members,

The above demonstrates a callous and grotesque disregard for the inherent human rights and human dignity of African-Americans. In terms of the exhaustion of domestic remedy, President Bill Clinton's withdrawal of Lani Guiniers's nomination as Assistant Attorney General for Civil Rights represents yet one more instance of the U.S. government's refusal to respond to continuing efforts on the part of African-Americans to achieve redress for past and on-going gross violations of human rights (see list of attempts, Appendix J). Concurrent with and responding to the failure of domestic efforts, African-Americans have addressed their grievances to the international community for decades (see list of precious initiatives, Appendix K). The forwarding of the April 30, 1992 IHRAAM Petition to the U.N. Sub-Commission by its Working Group, marked the first successful attempt to achieve

U.N. acceptance and consideration of such a communication addressing the question of past and on-going gross violations of African-Americans rights. That the U.S., in that instance, missed U.N. condemnation by only one vote, provides an indication of the high measure of agreement felt by the international community with regard to the arguments and charges expressed therein. However, U.N. consideration of the IHRAAM Petition is not enough. The Nation of Islam puts forward this Petition as a demand for action on African-American grievances by the Sub-Commission. Its failure to act appropriately will give the wrong message to the African-Americans, to the U.S. and to the world.

The U.S. government should not be given the tacit approval of the U.N. to continue to ignore past gross violations without compensation, nor to continue present gross violations against its national minorities. Surely, Members of the Sub-Commission, it is not your position nor that of the U.N., while situated in New York and surrounded by more than one million oppressed national minority members, to ignore their desperate plight, and at the same time assist U.S. human rights efforts in other countries. Surely, Mr. Secretary General and Sub-Commission Members, your position and that of the U.N. cannot be that in the U.S. only "white Americans" have internationally protected human rights, and that what is done to African-Americans does not count. The Nation of Islam is sure that this is not your position, nor that of the U.N.

Therefore:

In the name of African-American people, who are in full possession of their inherent human rights, the Nation of Islam calls upon the U.N. to intervene in favor of a sincere dialogue on the issues of reparations and self determination, and to act as a third party in setting up the situation wherein such a dialogue can occur. The African-American people do not believe that an honest, truly useful and equitable solution can be achieved without a significant degree of U. N. assistance. African-American history is filled with attempts at trying to achieve a sincere dialogue with the majority Government. All attempts to achieve domestic remedies have failed. In 400 years, African-Americans have not even come close to achieving equal-status relations with the Anglo-American majority ethnarchy which controls and runs the U.S. government as it sees fit, claims and distributes socio-economic resources as it sees fit, and ignores the human rights of African-Americans when it sees fit, etc.

Now African-Americans want their human rights, demands for equal status, self determination, and compensation for past and on-going gross violations to be heard and redressed, and are requesting U.N. assistance. This can be accomplished by observers being sent to the U.S., by an investigative committee, by a special rapporteur's investigation, by the opening of a forum at the U.N. wherein any and all sectors of the African-American community and the U.S. government will be able, without fear of retaliation, to express their grievances on the issues of self-determination and reparation for past and on-going gross violations of their human rights, and seek U. N. assistance in defining and resolving the crisis in this relation which has proved so destructive, not just to African-Americans, but to America as a whole. In this endeavor, the U.N. can expect the full cooperation and assistance of the Nation of Islam, and the vast majority of other African-American groups and individuals.

Members of the Sub-Commission:

African-Americans demand only those remedies that have been afforded to all other peoples or minorities, including the the indigenous peoples and minorities of most developed countries. If the U.S. government is sincere about dealing honestly and candidly with human rights problems of its African-American population, then it should not object to this time-honored process of third party (U.N.) assistance, mediation, conciliation or arbitration.

The Nation of Islam recalls:

At the beginning of their history in America, the enslaved Africans brought to America were defined in the same terms as the cattle belonging to the Anglo-American rulers. Thus, they were educated and socialized to accept that only the Anglo-American government could deal with their oppression. However convenient it was for the U.S. rulers, that time is now passe'. The African-American national minority is now emerging from the period of political domestification. It is only normal that it now begins, in addition to looking towards the majority government, to look towards the U.N. and the international community for technical, political and economic assistance. The U.N. cannot continue to ignore the oppression of national minorities in its host country, and still maintain it's human rights credibility in the World.

The Nation of Islam salutes you, Mr. Secretary-General and Members of the Sub-Commission, and looks forward to a prompt reply. The African-American people continue to suffer as they have over the past 400 years of their unending struggle in the U.S. (See Appendix E) against gross human rights violations. The Nation of Islam request U.N. attention to this on-going problem of gross violations of the human rights of African-Americans without apology and compensation and in particular, to the present flagrant violation of the rights of African-Americans to special measures or affirmative action, which is viewed with such fear and rejection in the U.S. as to occasion the withdrawal of the nomination of Lani Guinier as Assistant Attorney General for Civil Rights.

The Nation of Islam recommends the opening of a forum (perhaps under the auspices of the Sub-Commission), similar to the one opened for Aboriginal peoples in Geneva so that African-American human rights grievances that form the basis of the present petition can be expressed, systematically and officially recorded, evaluated and remedied.

To achieve this hearing, the Nation of Islam looks forward to cooperation with the U.N. and the U.S. government to facilitate the success of an appropriate forum.

Sincerely,

Silis Muhammad

Chief Executive Officer of

The Lost-Found Nation of Islam

LIST OF APPENDICES

APPENDIX A: Detroit death of a black motorist

"Detroit's Brutal Lessons," *Newsweek*, November 30, 1992

"Cops on Trial," *Time*, November 30, 1982

"Ex-Officers in Detroit Guilty in Beating Death of Motorist," *New York Times,* August 24th, 1992

APPENDIX B: Historical Judicial Bias in U.S. Courts

Excerpts from Y. N. Kly, *The Anti-Social Contract,* Clarity Press, Atlanta, 1989

APPENDIX C: Contemporary Status of Civil Rights/Non-Discrimination in U. S. Courts

"The Court, Still Haggling Over Rights, "*New York Times,* June 14, 1989

"A Changed Court Revises Rules on Civil Rights," *New York Times,* June 18, 1989

Excerpts from "On Being Overly Discreet and Insular: Involuntary Groups and the Anglo-American Judicial Tradition," by Aviam Soifer, Dean of Law, Boston College, in *The Protection of*

Minorities and Human Rights, ed. Yoram Dinstein and Mala Tabory, 1992

Excerpts from "Sins of Discrimination: Last Term's Affirmative Action Cases", by Kathleen M. Sullivan, Assistant Professor of Law, Harvard Law School, in *Harvard Law Review;* Vol. 100, No 1, Nov. 86

APPENDIX D: History of Slavery

"The African Slave Trade," *National Geographic,* September, 1992

APPENDIX E: African-American Resistance

"Chronology of U. S. Slave Rebellions and Conspiracies, 1663-1863," *The Negro Almanac: A Reference Work on the African-American, 5th Edition.* Compiled edited by Perry A. Plooskie and James Williams, Gale Research Inc., Detroit, 1989

Excerpts from the presentation of the Malcolm X Grassroots Movement before an African-American Community Hearing on Human Rights Violations, June 7-10, 1990

APPENDIX F: Evidence of Murder, Torture and Violence Against African-Americans

Chapter titled "The Evidence," from *We Charge Genocide,* 1960

Excerpts from Communication to the U. N. Commission on Human Rights titled "Human Rights Violations by the Police Against Blacks in the U. S. A.", submitted by A. Ray McCoy, June 10, 1982 and June 29, 1983. Document prepared by the Coalition Against Police Abuse, Los Angeles

APPENDIX G: Documentation of U. S. Government's Political Intimidation and harrassment of African-American Leadership and Population

"Well, Not So Extraordinary: Spy Networks II," *The Nation*, May 3, 1993

Presidential Review Memorandum/NSC-46, Zbigniew Brezinski, Carter Administration, 1978

"Amnesty Int'l target racist use of death penalty", *Workers World*, April 26, 1987

Letter re Operation Weed and Seed, American Civil Liberties Union of Washington, March 26, 1992

APPENDIX H: Indices of African-American Inequality

"U. S. Imprisons Black Men at 4 times S. Africa's Rate", *L. A. Times,* January 5, 1991

"Anger Over Racism is Seen as a Cause of Blacks High Blood Pressure", *New York Times,* April 24, 1990

"White Families' Wealth Put at 10 Times Blacks", *L. A. Times,* January 11, 1991

"The Death Gap: Life expectancy for blacks decreases to 69.2 but stands at 75.6 for whites"

Disproportionality of African-American Involvement in the Criminal Justice System

Statistical and other citations, *The Negro Almanac: A Reference Work on the African-American, 5th Edition.* Compiled and edited by Perry A. Plooskie and James Williams, Gale Research Inc., Detroit, 1989, (67 pages).

APPENDIX I: The Guinier Nomination

NAACP Bulletin, July 30, 1993

Compilation of articles from *The New York Times*

"Getting Guinier", *The Nation,* May 31, 1993

"The Voting Rights Act: A Troubled Past," *Newsweek,* June 14, 1993

"Withdraw Guinier," *The New Republic,* June 14, 1993

"The Turning", *The New Republic,* June 28, 1993

"Clinton's Drift Left on Civil Rights has Business Edgy," *Business Week*; May 31, 1993

APPENDIX J: African-American Efforts to Achieve Domestic Remedy

APPENDIX K: African-American Initiatives to the International Community

2014 Open Letter to U.S. President Barack Obama

Silis Muhammad of the Lost-Found Nation of Islam's Open Letter to U.S. President Obama Requesting Reparations For Slavery

Need for Reparations for Slavery Urgent Due to Imminent Doom of America
Silis Muhammad, Lost-Found Nation of Islam Chief Executive Officer, released a letter dated January 15, 2014 that was sent to U.S. President Barack Obama requesting reparations for slavery.

Along with U.S. President Obama, the letter was addressed to Congress, the Joint Chief of Staff, and the Pope of Rome, urging America to honor its reparations obligations to Afrodescendants. Hundreds of people have signed Reparations Petitions (digitally and on paper) preceding release of the Open Letter.

"We, the undersigned, urgently request sea-going and air-going ships or vessels and freeway, highway, bridge, and road-building materials and equipment," said Mr. Muhammad in the letter.
Mr. Muhammad released the letter on February 23, 2014 in Atlanta during his address at the Lost-Found Nation of Islam's Saviors Day Celebration, themed "The Blueprint". Click here to read Mr. Muhammad's open letter to President Obama and others. Sign the Reparations Petition located on the North American Reparations Taskforce's (NARTF) website here.

"We are asking for equipment to cultivate land. We need materials and machinery with which to make clothing, shoes, and furniture and we need materials and equipment for putting in infrastructure," the letter reads.Read the full letter to President Obama and others. Sign the Reparations Petition located on the NARTF's website here.

"We want housing, apartments, and multi-story building materials and equipment. In addition, we ask for the cost of a one-way ticket to whatever islands that would accept us as full citizens.

Whether the Government of America will or will not give this, we not less than 144,000 of us, are determined to leave America and live amongst our own kind."

The Lost-Found Nation of Islam currently spearheads a growing number of initiatives to advance Afrodescendant ethnogenesis, human rights, and self-determination. Printed petitions can be signed at any Lost-Found Nation of Islam mosque here.

If you're a supporter of reparations and would like to see Afrodescendants receive reparations for slavery, the ebook entitled "42 Ways To Show Support For Reparations and Afrodescendant Human Rights" will help you to help make that happen and more! Check it out {FREE} here:Here's How You Can Play A BIG Part In Helping To Claim Reparations For Transatlantic Slavery | North American Reparations Taskforce . You may also make a donation here

Posted in Lost-Found Nation of Islam,Reparations for Slavery

Silis Muhammad
CHIEF EXECUTIVE OFFICER
THE LOST-FOUND NATION OF ISLAM

TO: President Barack Obama, President of the United States
U.S. Congress
General Martin E. Dempsey, Joint Chief of Staff
Pope of Rome

FROM: Silis Muhammad

RE: THE BLUEPRINT: OUR PLAN FOR AMERICA AND ITS AFRODESCENDANTS

DATE: January 15, 2014

The peoples and Governments of the world are well aware of the duplicity of the United States Government as it calls for Human Rights and democracy while continuing, to this day, systematic discrimination against and disenfranchisement of its Afrodescendant population--the inheritors of the legacy of plantation slavery (the so-called African Americans). While we recognize that moral leadership is the tone that the United States Government wishes to convey to the world, it as failed to take the key moral action that would begin to repair the ongoing wrong that has existed since the very inception of this government. Does anyone recognize the significance of this key to peace?

I am Silis Muhammad, Chief Executive Officer of the Lost-found Nation of Islam. If we could summon the hatred our ancestors had for this Caucasian American Government and bring that condition to bear on the shoulders of this generation of Afrodescendants the resulting wrath would be like unto a blaze of fire, the size of which would engulf the United States. It would burn for 1,000 years! The evil done to the Black man by the American government far surpasses the evil done by any other Government, especially the Governments of France, Germany, Great Britain, and Canada.

We are determined to leave America, not less than 144,000 of us, Arfodescendants. We, the children of plantation slavery, were subsumed by the thirteenth and fourteenth amendments of the Constitution of the United States of America, which does not, in the least, express our will. We want no part of the prophesied imminent doom of America.

We want the United States, in cooperation with the International Monetary Fund, to arrange for forgiveness of all debts owed by St. Kitts and all other members of CARICOM, who would welcome, with full citizenship, appropriate numbers of educated and industrious Afrodescendants from the United States. We are asking for sea-going and air-going ships or vessels and freeway, highway, bridge, and road building materials and equipment. We are asking for equipment to cultivate land. We need materials and machinery with which to make clothing, shoes, and furniture and we need materials and equipment to for putting in infrastructure. We want housing, apartments, and multi-story building materials and equipment. In addition, we ask for the cost of a one-way ticket to whatever islands that would accept us as full citizens.Whether the Government of America will or will not give this, we, not less than 144,000 of us, are determined to leave America and live amongst our own kind.

The American Government gives billions of dollars to Israel each year. It has committed to giving Haiti $20-million per year for the next four years, for food. In addition, she gives to Haiti and other countries her surplus old clothing, foods, and machinery. Will she give to her ex-plantation slave children our request of her? Abraham Lincoln stated, "keep them here as our underlings." We, today, observe daily that we are treated and kept as underlings here in America. The images of how we are looked upon by this Caucasian American Government are yet on our minds and in our lives today.

The killing of Travon Martin in 2013 is a prime example, of which the world is well aware. Yet, perhaps the greatest example of the systematic immorality of the United States Government is her claim to the largest prison population in the world--prisons filled with Black men and women due to discriminatory policing, prosecution, and laws. There is no justice here. We are subjected to an ongoing slavery system--slavery by another name. The world can see that you are not our brothers and neither are we yours.

The ex-slave masters of the CARICOM countries have departed and left the Governments in the hands of their ex-slaves. What has this American Government given to her plantation slave children besides a subservient position as her underlings?

Psychiatrists and those in other related sciences say if a husband hits or beats his wife, his wife is to leave him immediately. Has the American government not done far worse to us, Afrodescendants? We have been whipped until blood gushed from our backs, boiled while yet alive until dead, and hung from trees: to say nothing of the cruelest of inhumane treatments. The loss of our mother tongue, culture, and religion renders us a spiritually dead nation. . These are losses of Human Rights as defined by Article 27 of the ICCPR of the United Nations.

We, the Lost-Found Nation of Islam, have been in the International community since 1989. Our first written statement to the U.N. was in 1993. Our first oral statement to the U.N. was in

1998. Our last statement and appearance in the U.N. was in 2006. We spoke to the Commission on Human Rights, the Sub-Commission on the Promotion and Protection of Human Rights, and the Working Group on Minorities and had significantly gained their attention. But the American Government along with the British Government , the Governments of all slave-holding countries and other countries whom Britain and America provide support, shut down the Commission on Human Rights, the Sub-Commission on the Promotion and Protection of Human Rights, and the Working Group on Minorities--every U.N. group whose attention we had gained. In its place, they created the Human Rights Council.

We spent nine years in the U.N. only to learn that we did not exist as a Nation of people, with God-given human rights. As Americans, we were classified along with Caucasian Americans in the United States. We had achieved a unified name and identity that Black people from 19 countries agreed upon, in 2002--Afrodescendants. God-given Human Rights are: the right to speak your own mother tongue in community with others who speak your mother tongue; the right to practice your own culture in community with others who practice your culture; and the right to practice your own religion in community with others who practice your religion Our Human Rights were lost during plantation slavery. This American government made us a debased people. This is why this letter is presented to the President of the United States and the United States Government. We are determined to achieve ethnogenesis.

The following is a statement of American history. Henry Louis Gates, Jr. wrote "The Truth Behind 40 Acres and a Mule," on pbs.org's '100 Amazing facts About The Negro'.

January 16, 1865, Union General William T. Sherman issued Special Field Order No. 15, upon approval of President Lincoln: "The islands from Charleston, South Carolina, the abandoned rice fields along the rivers for thirty miles back from the sea, and the country bordering the St. Johns River, Florida, are reserved and set apart for the settlement of the negros now made free by the acts of war and the proclamation of the President of the United States (Abraham Lincoln).

400,000 acres of land--a strip of coastline stretching from Charleston, South Carolina, to the St. Johns River in Florida, including Georgia's Sea Islands and the mainland thirty miles from the coast--would be redistributed to the newly freed slaves.

For the first time in the history of this nation, the representatives of the Government had gone to these poor debased people to ask them what they wanted for themselves.

Baptist minister Ulysses L. Houston, one of the group that had met with Sherman led 1,000 Blacks to Skidaway Island, Georgia where they established a self-governing community with Houston as the "Black governor." And by June, 40,000 freedmen had settled on 400,000 acres of "Sherman Land." By the way, Sherman later ordered that the army could lend the new settlers mules; hence the phrase "40 acres and a mule."

What happened to this astonishingly visionary program, which would have fundamentally altered the course of American race relations?

Henry Louis Gates, Jr. goes on to say:

Andrew Johnson, Lincoln's successor and a sympathizer with the South, overturned the Order in the fall of 1865, and, as Barton Myers sadly concluded, 'returned the land along the South Carolina, Georgia, and Florida coasts to the planters who had originally owned it--to the very people who had declared war on the United States of America.'

The Honorable Elijah Muhammad, along with 450,000 followers, from 1960 until the day of his death in 1975, repeatedly asked this Government to establish a state or territory of our own. The American Government turned a deaf ear. Is there not a moral-minded Caucasian in America's Government today? In 1865, we have in evidence at least two moral-minded statesmen: the United States President, Abe Lincoln, and General Sherman. They, at least, possessed enough moral insight to inquire of the new allegedly free Blacks what it is they wanted: "To live scattered amongst Whites or to live separate?" "Land" was the Black soon-to-be governors answer. Moreover, the Black soon-to-be governor stated, "there is a prejudice against us in the South. We would rather live in a separate territory." To date, the majority of Black people everywhere in the United States still experience this prejudice.

Is the Government of the United States incapable of the moral fortitude that it would take to grant to not less than 144,000 souls our humble request? Is there not one white man in the Government today, who has the wisdom, moral fortitude, and leadership ability of General Sherman and Abraham Lincoln? Ease the souls of my people, as well as make clean the souls of white people, by correcting your nation's wrongs. You claim that your nation has has changed, but our lawyers, doctors, teachers, and people feel your nation's prejudices even today.

To quote my daughter, Amira Arshad Muhammad, who is an attorney: "We are the peace that the world has been waiting for." You know what is right to do; just do it. Nature equips you from birth with the knowledge of what is right and what is wrong. You know more about our history than the majority of us do, for it was your government that placed us in plantation slavery, debased us, and made us your underlings. Men and governments advance in age and in wisdom. Has your government advanced in wisdom, or does it lag behind?

About The Author

Silis Muhammad is the Chief Executive Officer (CEO) of the Lost-Found Nation of Islam. Mr. Muhammad nurtures spiritual life within the Afrodescendant people worldwide using a Divine understanding of the teachings of the Most Honorable Elijah Muhammad (peace be upon him), knowledge of civil death, his expertise in international law (human rights and reparations), and an undying love for Afrodescendant people.

Mr. Muhammad first joined the Nation of Islam in Los Angeles after hearing a Minister of the Messenger teach, where something indescribable rested well with his soul upon listening at that time. Mr. Muhammad was very much active in the L.A. Temple from 1962 forward, although he did not have an official position until 1964. He had a cordial relationship with the Minister of the Mosque, and his relationship was even friendlier with the Captain of the Mosque. During that friendship, Mr. Muhammad developed a gratitude for the masculine qualities that the Captain displayed, and for the image that he projected for a young man like himself. In 1964, Mr. Muhammad was raised to the position of Captain of the west coast during the First Resurrection of the Nation of Islam over Muhammad Speaks, by the Honorable Elijah Muhammad. That position and function took him all across the west coast into every Temple. During that time, Mr. Muhammad married his wife Harriett, who is an ex-daughter-in-law of the Most Honorable Elijah Muhammad.

After the physical death of the Most Honorable Elijah Muhammad, Mr. Muhammad resurrected the Lost-Found Nation of Islam in 1977. As a result, Founder's Day is recognized on August 21st of each year. As CEO of the Lost-Found Nation of Islam and All for Reparations & Emancipation (AFRE), Mr. Muhammad works day and night to give Afrodescendants the knowledge and resources required to gain 100% freedom, justice, and equality, recognition and restoration of their human rights…and to bring about self-determination.

Mr. Muhammad has spent more than 30+ years teaching Afrodescendants (so-called African-Americans) the basis of their problem, civil death, and its solution. Mr. Muhammad has authored a growing library, filled with wisdom, on civil death and human rights of Afrodescendants to add to the highly valued knowledge left by the Most Honorable Elijah Muhammad
.

NOTE:

NOTES:

Made in the USA
Columbia, SC
24 April 2024

ec2b48f0-9d44-4293-8a18-903e116a31b2R02